DEDICATION

For my precious wife Candy and our daughters Jessica and Emily
with the intention of providing a clear and ever-present Daymark in
their lifetime journey downstream.

Introduction

I want to thank you for taking the time to pick up this book. If you only use it to line a bird cage, build a fire after falling in the River or for any other use you might have for paper in the great outdoors at least the tree these words are printed on didn't die in vain.

Don't think for a minute that the author of this baby is a tree-hugging kind of guy. The only time I hug a tree is on the way up to a platform stand some 20 feet off the ground. Trees seem to grow a lot faster than they did 20 years ago. Maybe they just seem taller because the thought that falling and getting really, really hurt crosses my mind more frequently than those days when I made a living running into burning buildings and working as a paramedic.

A primary focus of my life has always been the outdoors, which was literally out my back door growing up at the edge of town in little Mt. Carroll, Illinois back in the 1950's and '60's.

The honesty of the outdoors brought considerably more comfort than the company of others as a child. Most of the kids I grew up with learned the value of coloring between the lines.

Why would anybody even want to pick up crayons when Carroll Creek beckoned with bullfrogs, bullheads and the lack of general B.S. of finding your place as another brick in the wall?

In the Mt. Carroll High School yearbook Waukarusa classmates tasked with describing young Teddy Peck wrote "It takes all kinds to make a world". Those kids had wisdom and insight far beyond their years.

You'll meet a lot of characters in the course of reading this book. Most names have been changed to protect the innocent, the clueless and a few co-conspirators who have greatly enriched the tapestry of my life.

One of these folks is called Mike Blart in this book. He is a giant of a man with incredible insight if given the time to think things through. On several occasions Blart has accused me of following my own program rather than going with the general flow of events.

Guilty as charged. Blart is this way, too. So are a couple more of my closest friends. Blart played pro football for a living. This livelihood required following somebody else's program with precision timing.

I was a professional firefighter for 22 years. The only lesson learned from this experience was that the chief may not always be right—but he's still the chief. I spent a considerable amount of time in the chief's office explaining why my behavior did not fall between guidelines others had little trouble following in a long blue line dating back to the late 1800's.

Emergency scenes were never a problem. They tell me I've always been a good man in a storm. Co-conspirator "Dan Wabasha" and I were like a couple of playful otters forced to work with a unit of serious beavers. Supervisors tried their best to keep us from working together, perhaps resenting the fact that we had too much fun.

When the fire was out or the critically ill patient had his pulse restored, life around the firehouse was usually too mundane. There may be another book floating around about firehouse life in the nether reaches of my brain. It may stay there next to several lesions which the doctor said probably resulted from blunt force trauma from bouncing along on the roller coaster of life.

That's the thing about life. You don't know where it will take you or how long you have to play. If it suddenly ended tomorrow I would have no complaints. Somewhere between the slow crawl up that first stretch of track and the loop-de-loops which follow I accepted Christ as my personal savior. I know where eternity will be spent.

Folks who share my boat will likely hear this message and some other stories about life on the River. Both sides of my family have lived near this aortic artery of the heartland since Civil War days.

One ancestor on my mother's side was an engineer for the Grand Army of the Republic. When he mustered out he was given a tract of land near Prairie du Chien, Wisconsin where he had a hand in building one of the first bridges over the Upper Mississippi.

Another ancestor by marriage on my father's side worked as a surveyor, plotting LeClaire and Davenport, Iowa before moving up to Carroll County, Illinois This epiphany came to light as part of research by a man named John Elliott who was moved to investigate family genealogy. In the course of this work Johnny discovered we were cousins.

Johnny put me back in touch with my first cousin, Professor Jimbo Peck. Few persons call this botanist who has spent over 31 years at the University of Arkansas "Jimbo".

This is what I called Cousin Jim the last time I saw him back in 1965, more than half a lifetime ago. Since then we've begun rekindling family heritage. Jimbo has discovered he has a couple of nieces and nephews. The nieces are my kids, Jessica and Emily.

Both of my girls grew up in the outdoors, with early experiences having both subtle and profound influence as they move along the river of life.

Until the summer of 2010 I didn't know my paternal grandfather had a half brother. Some day my daughters may wonder exactly where they plug into the cosmic scheme of things.

The main thrust of this book is to make accessing the past a little easier for them when they reach this point in life. The Mississippi River has been a common thread in my life and the lives of my ancestors. It was on the bank of this Grand River that I asked Candy Law to be my wife back in 1971.

The Old Guy—my Dad—said marrying Candy and a career as a firefighter for the City of Beloit, Wisconsin were the two smartest things I ever did. The Old Guy "went down the chute" in 1991. I think about him almost every day. He is still right by my side, only in a different dimension.

There comes a point in every man's life when the chute comes over the horizon. You may get there in an instant accompanied by squealing tires and breaking glass. You may just fade away at some "wrinkle ranch" where some doctor who really doesn't want to be there tells a 22-year-old she can stop squeezing the bag connected to a tube sticking down your throat, droning to another dispassionate observer the official time of death.

Only God knows the time and place when we become a memory. My final wish is to have my ashes scattered on my beloved Mississippi at a time and place those left behind deem appropriate without feeling compelled to ask anyone's permission.

To date there have been few regrets. The future holds but one true fear: that my wife will sell my guns and fishing gear for what I told her I paid for the stuff. Hope you enjoy the book.

"Good cat!"

Contents

The Old Guy

You wouldn't be reading these words if it weren't for the Old Guy. All who knew my Dad said he was a real piece of work. He was a small man, maybe 5'9" and 150 pounds soaking wet.

The Old Guy was never afraid to get soaking wet, if that's what the situation called for. This might mean stripping down to skivvies to retrieve a duck which fell in water just a little too deep for hippers or jumping into a backwater slough to tussle with a big catfish which had spent all night weaving the limb line it was hooked to amongst tangled roots of a sprawling river maple.

One of his most admirable traits was integrity. He was a man of principle and spine whose mantra was "Be sure you are right, then

1

go ahead." Once a decision was made the Old Guy became a force of nature not unlike the Mississippi –essentially unstoppable, regardless of what waited downstream.

Like many of the generation who put their lives on hold to save humanity in World War II, Herb Peck was slow to show emotion or sympathy. He knew life was tough and that the world was not about to stop and give some doofus a break or a "do over." Mistakes required immediate payment in full. The reward was wisdom in not making the same mistake twice.

The old guy played me like a big bass on a very light line, knowing exactly when to give and when to take, resulting in a passion for the outdoors which still knows no bounds.

He had the same passion in those steely grey-green eyes until the day that he died. Sometimes they burned with the intensity of purpose. Other times they danced with laughter, often at my expense. More often than not our vision was focused on some facet of the amazing virtual classroom of the Mighty Mississippi.

Back before I became part of the equation the Old Guy and his lifelong buddy Bill Bower had an old railroad boxcar which had been converted into a cabin overlooking Sand Slough on Pool 13.

He managed to hold on to this vestige of Manland after Bower moved away, including me in escapes from anything that might keep him from the outdoors at a very early age.

I must have been about five years old when Bower came back to visit, with designs of going jug fishing a little later in the day.

Jug fishing is so simple a five year old can do it. Catching fish is little more than the basic maneuver of lifting the jug, 18 inches of heavy nylon line and the fish at the other end into a leaky wooden boat.

The only thing lacking in bringing this plan to fruition was a shortage of serviceable jugs. Fortunately, Bower had shown up with 24 of them—brown 12 ounce bottles which needed to have Blatz beer removed before being corked and put into service.

The Old Guy and Bower said it would take awhile to get the gear ready for jug fishing, directing me to take a cane pole and can of worms down by the leaky wooden boat to practice in the sleepy duck-weed covered waters of Sand slough.

A huge bass felt like eating worms that afternoon and did everything she could to pull the cane pole out of my tiny hands. The Old Guy and Bower responded to my little girlish squeals in an instant, ready to tangle with the big snake or giant snapping turtle which was apparently threatening my life.

Dad grabbed the cane pole with one hand while using the other to push me out of the way, right into a patch of horse nettles. The nettles were a mere footnote to the trauma which came next.

It only took a couple of seconds for the Old Guy to determine this fish was too big to land by conventional means. With no explanation or apparent concern for the little boy flailing in the nettle patch, he let the bass take that cane pole right out of his hand, plowing across the duckweed of Sand slough.

If Johnny Stewart could have recorded the sounds I made next those who chase coyotes and similar critters would never need to buy another predator call. It must have sounded like a cross between a wounded rabbit and a young crow which had just fallen 40 feet out of the nest and landed on its head.

Somehow the Old Guy was able to growl "Shadd-up!" with even more decibels than I was emitting without losing the Lucky Strike

"The Old Guy with Lake Erie Walleyes—1980."

cigarette clenched between his lips.

"Git in the boat!" he grunted with the very next breath. Bower was already manning the oars with an ear to ear grin splayed across his big, bald face. My skin was starting to itch from tumbling in the nettles as I sniffled to the stern bench seat as ordered.

Bower skillfully directed the square stern of the leaky wooden boat towards my cane pole which was quivering with life beside a mat of heavy weeds.

"Pick up the damn pole, kid," the Old Guy groaned. Bower's big body quaked with laughter, emitting spontaneous sneezy snorts of unfettered glee.

Every living thing in Sand slough had to hear the commotion echoing from that boat when I swung 18 inches of pungent green bass over the gunwale of that rowboat.

Both men knew that the twig of my lifeline had been bent forever. I did not know it then, but the tail of what would eventually become a full-fledged River Rat was twitching with excitement.

Ten years later the Old Guy sat patiently in the shade of a red oak puffing on his Lucky Strike as I bailed water from the back of another leaky wooden boat up at Uncle Howard's slough near the confluence of Apple River with the Mississippi at the edge of the old Savanna Army Depot.

It was May and the crappies were piling tight against certain stumps and tangles to spawn like they have done almost forever.

A south wind was howling down the slough, creating whitecaps on what was normally quiet water. The Old Guy said I should pace my bailing activity because it would take a fair amount of stamina and endurance to row the leaky wooden boat a mile or so down to a fork in the backwater that was a perennial spring crappie magnet where we could fish pretty much out of the wind.

He announced it was time to go with a couple of inches of water still sloshing around in the bottom of the boat. I grabbed my cane poles, my Old Pal tackle box and Dad's crappie rod out of our '61 Chevy BelAir and stowed them along the gunwale.

Dad lit another smoke and got comfortable on the stern seat as I pulled hard on the oars. It takes awhile to row a mile into the wind in a leaky wooden boat. Dad got his crappie rod ready directing me to pull a little harder on the right or left oar from time to time to ensure we were following the most direct course to those treasured stumps.

The Old Guy's favorite crappie rig was a telescoping metal panfish pole with about fifty feet of black Dacron line wrapped around a rickety brass fly reel. This outfit was known as the "Thin Winder" for as long as I can remember, so named because the reel's dimensions were different than the Pflueger Supreme baitcast reels of his other prized fishing outfits.

He would never let me use any of his gear. My weapon was a three-piece cane pole which he said — with total accuracy — was "the best fish catchin' sumbitch you can use on the River." This description still holds true in this age of high modulus graphite rods.

By age 13 I had amassed enough resources from mowing lawns and shoveling snow to possess three sumbitches, one of which I was honored to let the Old Guy use when we were chasing crappies.

Looking back to the genesis of the Thin Winder, I believe this crappie rod was so named to keep me from confusing it with the bait cast outfits back in the days before I could differentiate between the two and the Old Guy decided it was time for me to fetch the gear so we could go fishin'.

We were still a good quarter mile away from the special stumps when the Old Guy's desire to fish goaded him into action. He must have bailed four or five loads out of the one pound metal Hills Bros. coffee can in the home stretch while chiding me to row faster.

Finally, we arrived at the stumps and secured the boat with manila rope at both ends.

"Where are the minnows?" The Old Guy asked almost sheepishly. My mind flashed back to Dad waiting patiently under that oak tree puffing on his smoke. Next to him were his tackle box and a Falls River minnow bucket with a removable liner.

Dad read my mind, as was often the case as he watched me stumble through life. He made no apologies for forgetting the bait bucket. When it was time to fish I was supposed to remember everything needed to find success.

"If you don't have it in your head, you've gotta have it in your feet, boy!" he barked. "We can't catch fish without minnows. Guess we need to go back."

The return trip to the shady oak only took a few minutes, pushed by both wind and desire. Getting back to the stumps was a little tougher. When we finally tied the boat up and the Old Guy plopped his big red and white Dayton float next to some always productive wood. My shoulders ached and there were blisters on the palms of both hands.

This was no time to dwell on discomfort. " Ooooh! This one is an Eachy Peach" he chuckled, sweeping a 13 inch silver slab into the boat.

We used to have an old pontoon boat built out of plywood and 55 gallon oil drums tied up along the River on the north side of Savanna. Later that summer The Old Guy let me take her out alone while he probably spent the afternoon evaluating new equipment for jug fishing.

The following year these forays morphed into trips of several days duration, probing backwaters of Pool 13 by day and camping on Santa Fe sandbar at night.

I had my first guide job working from that pontoon boat that summer. It was my seventh grade teacher Mr. Ogle and his Dad. I was paid $25 for the trip—a fortune to a fifteen year old kid.

The Old Guy smiled when I showed him the money. He smiled a lot from that point forward, laughing out loud when I finally figured out the Old Guy was really now an Old Guy with all the rights and privileges of one who has passed the torch to the next generation of River Rats.

"Keepin' it real."

Rules and Regulations

River rats generally just want to be left alone. I believe we could function quite well by merely following the golden rule: Treat others the way you would like to be treated.

This imperative and my Dad's mantra "Be sure you're right, then go ahead" are still at the core of my personal beliefs. I still chafe at authority, maybe because the powers that be never included me in a rules meeting.

The Old Guy saw wisdom in letting me learn from mistakes, at times finding considerable amusement at this education process.

Sixty years into the Game of Life I'm still just about one rule or regulation away from getting serious about the South Beach Diet, consuming copious amounts of melatonin and joining the Somali pirates.

Permit for my AK-47? NO I DON'T HAVE A PERMIT FOR MY AK-47! I DON'T HAVE ONE FOR THIS RPG, EITHER. WHAT ARE YOU GONNA DO ABOUT IT?

The next little constraint on my freedom will probably be a small one. Options will be weighed and I will fall in line with the rest of the American Sheeple. But one of these days....

This defiant streak manifested at a fairly early age. Quotes by my name in the Mt. Carroll High School yearbook Waukarusa are "Rules are made to be broken" and "It takes all kinds to make a world".

You won't find my senior mug shot in the Waukarusa. There is a line drawing of a little kid chasing a school bus where the photo ought to be, with Ted Peck : Photo not available beneath this cartoon.

I was not about to wear a coat and tie to get a photo taken when the professional photographer came to the school to take official yearbook pictures. Back then we don't go to fancy studios like kids do today. We posed for mug shots. Front view, no side view.

My folks were not amused when they found out I did not participate in Picture Day. A make-up day was scheduled. Dad gave me $3 to get the job done. Being just one of two or three kids wearing a coat and tie amongst a bunch of other fish in my year class wearing jeans was an obvious opportunity involving ridicule which would result in at least one fist fight and another trip to the principal's office.

Not wanting to subject one of my classmates to both a fat lip and discipline, I ditched school with my buddy Randy Richter. We used the $3 Dad had forked over for the mandatory mug shot to buy snacks and bait. Then we went fishin'.

Since we're already on a nostalgia tangent, a word about kids bringing guns to school is in order. I grew up in town with cornfields and woods a two minutes sneak out the back door.

Childhood pal Bobby Williams lived on a farm that had pheasants running all over the place. He invited me to stay over night and do a little bird hunting. Mother just heard the part about staying over, probably because the lesson about not providing too much information to authority figures was already sinking in.

I walked to school that morning carrying a 20 gauge Remington 870 pumpgun in a cloth case. The gun and a box of #6 shot were stuffed in my locker and I joined the horde of other junior high kids on their way to class.

Miss McCarthy had hall duty that day. She was from the Chicago area and nothing short of stunning. Like many other boys about to rub their small antlers on the saplings of adolescence, I had a serious crush on Miss McCarthy.

In an effort to impress her I made a tiny coffin with little brass hinges and her name woodburned into the top in shop class. The last thing I ever wanted to do was break her heart.

When the loudspeaker announced I was to report forthwith to the office it took me by surprise. I was still mulling capers which hadn't been discovered yet and contemplating explanations when I saw Miss McCarthy sitting in a chair sobbing.

Mr. Gorsuch, the assistant principal, gestured for us both to enter his office. He had a large wooden paddle behind the desk with holes drilled in it. The holes were probably designed to minimize wind resistance when assuming the position for the "board of education".

"Teddy, did you bring a gun to school today?" Mr. Gorsuch asked.

"Yessir, I did," I replied.

"Why did you bring a gun to school," he asked with voice about two octaves higher.

"I was gonna go home with Bobby Williams and hunt pheasants after school," I said.

The principal smirked. Telling the truth is always a good thing, although there is much to be said for not telling the whole truth and nothing but the truth.

"Do you have a lock for your locker, Ted?"

" No sir, " I answered.

"Then bring your gun to the office. You can pick it up after school," the principal said. Miss McCarthy sat slack jawed.

"Cub" Zillhart, the school bus driver grinned when Bobby and I boarded the bus.

"Gonna go shoot some birds at Bobby's, huh," he said " I saw a big rooster by the mailbox when I was driving up there this morning," he winked "Give 'em hell!"

That's the way things were done in Carroll County back in the day.

My first run in with the law is a continuation of this theme. Paul "Sprink" Hensal was the local game warden. Back then there were only four wardens in all of northwest Illinois. Like the others, Sprink was a tough old bird.

There used to be a lot of rabbits hopping around Carroll County right after World War II. Before Sprink became a warden he used to ride around back roads at night with my Dad, other cronies, some alcohol and a .410 pistol.

Road hunting at night with a .410 pistol and a belly full of beer has never been nor ever will be legal.

Dad and the other good old boys didn't abandon this form of rural entertainment after Hensal pinned on the star. His move to authority figure simply made the game more interesting.

We used to have a farm in Stransky's bottoms not far from the Mississippi. Come fall mallards used to tornado in there by the thousands, working cornfields before returning to the River to rest.

Dad often hunted out of a pit blind dug chest deep at the highest part of the cornfield. Ducks working a cornfield always start by pitching in at the high point and waddling out from there.

The Old Guy would always pile couple bushels of corn 40 yards out from the pit in all four directions as reference for when the mallards would be in range. He used to shoot a Browning A-5 automatic. Pulling out the "plug" to allow two more shots was part of his game plan.

Baiting and hunting with an un-plugged gun were two of Sprink's favorite citations to write. Shooting after hours made it a three ticket trifecta. He never caught my Dad, even though he would make a serious effort at least once a week. They would frequently meet at Hadley's café south of town for coffee.

One time Sprink bought me pancakes and bacon, hoping to gain insight on how The Old Guy always avoided apprehension. Of course I never spilled the beans.

A gravel road snakes along the bottom of the bluff just east of Stransky's bottoms. You can see for miles with a good pair of binoculars. But farmer Andy Houzenga could see a car parked anywhere along the road without the need for optics.

12

When Sprink tried sneaking to a vantage point in his old green Plymouth, Andy would take notice and simply turn on the yard light on the barn. Dad would see the light, put the plug back in his Browning and quit hunting at the designated time with no more than a legal limit of greenheads.

I knew the program well by age 16. One November afternoon my buddy Gomer and I headed down to the farm for a little duck hunting. The birds were really moving. A couple of other hunters had trespassed to shoot the mallards which were working our corn. They had a pile of ducks. Greenheads were falling out of their coats.

I kicked them off of our farm. They crossed the fence to a farm where they must have had permission and fired their guns in the air every time a flock of mallards would come whistling in almost close enough to shoot.

They left the field at about sunset, the end of legal shooting time. Gomer and I had yet to fire our guns. Another bunch of mallards started working across the bottoms. We hunkered down and got ready.

Flames spewed from our gun barrels when we finally stood to shoot. The only duck to fall was a mallard drake which caught a full pattern of #6 shot right in the chest.

It was well after dark when we piled into Gomer's '51 Pontiac to drive up the lane to the gravel road at the base of the bluff.

When we reached the gravel road Hensal's green Plymouth came screaming up out of nowhere, oscillating red light on the dash announcing our capture. I glanced over towards the barn where the yard light blazed in all its glory.

The warden jumped from his car almost before it came to a stop and barked "All right you little son-of-a-bitch! What's your excuse this time?"

We were busted. At the time my only regrets were only getting one duck and being caught shooting after hours.

"I don't have a watch Sprink," I offered.

"How many ducks did you shoot?" he growled. I held up our one pulverized mallard drake, green head hanging by a thread. Hensal laughed from the soul.

"One duck? One lousy duck? Didn't your Dad ever teach you how to shoot?"

My humiliation knew no bounds. The warden confiscated our guns and sent us on our way. The family was eating supper when I stumbled through the door. "How was the hunt, son?" Dad asked while passing the potatoes to my sister The Bean.

"Hensal caught us shooting late," I mumbled, looking at the floor. "Did Andy forget to turn the yard light on?" he asked. I shook my head no without looking up.

"You ought to be ashamed of yourself. Not only did you get caught, you only shot one duck!"

I'm sure the phone conversation between the warden and my father which took place while Gomer and I made the sad trip home was colorful. Dad told me I was to report to Mr. Hensal's house at 8 a.m. the following morning. It was a Sunday which changed my life forever.

For the next two weekends I had to ride around with the game warden on patrol. This included one Friday night when he caught two more duck hunters who didn't have the benefit of a yard light to warn them.

Sprink Hensal became a great mentor, later providing advice

when I was faced with the choice of becoming either a game warden or a firefighter. He said "you go be a fireman, Ted...and be a good one. You like to hunt and fish too much to be a warden."

At the end of those two weeks I had a new appreciation for the outdoors resource with the heavy responsibility of always trying to do the right thing from that point forward. Hensal said if you always kept the best interests of the resource at heart you could never go wrong. Thirty years later his words of wisdom held true in an encounter with the Wisconsin DNR.

Sprink gave me back my gun . He also gave me a brand new Timex watch and a card with the legal shooting hours. "Now listen to me, you little son-of-a-bitch. No more excuses!" I've tried to follow the rules ever since. Especially his advice about doing the best thing for the resource.

Back in the 1990's Wisconsin faced a wildlife management problem called Chronic Wasting Disease, or CWD. Wildlife managers decided one solution was to cull the deer herd by issuing essentially unlimited harvest tags.

I shot nine or 10 deer that year, including several nice bucks. Meanwhile, my Lab Hanna Banana sat at home without an offer to go pheasant hunting. Those big brown Labrador eyes finally guilted me into a quick bird hunt on the public hunting grounds near Evansville.

We hadn't been in the field 10 minutes when we came across a 10 point buck with a little basket rack, so ill and emaciated that it had to struggle to lift its head. I walked back to the truck and called the local game warden, the DNR office and the wildlife biologist. Nobody answered the phone.

I still had a valid buck tag in the glove compartment, but no deer slugs—just birdshot loads. It was time to make a tough decision. Wisconsin wardens have a well deserved reputation for being ruthless. The term "Nazi" has been used when describing them on more than one occasion.

Just up the hill was an animal which was suffering and in great pain. Putting this deer out of its misery would mean breaking the law by using birdshot to put it down. I did what I believed to be the right thing, then tagged the buck and phoned the warden, DNR office and wildlife biologist again to inform them I would be taking the animal to a check station. All I got were answering machines.

I dumped the carcass in a ditch on a buddy's farm, cutting off the rack as a reminder and tribute to this deer's life. The next day warden Shawna Stringham called, ordering me to report immediately to the local DNR office. She told me to bring the deer with me.

I told her where she could find the carcass and showed up as directed with the little rack. Warden Boyt Ridley was present, as was warden Stringham. They may have been playing 'good cop-bad cop' during the subsequent interrogation. If this was the case warden Ridley did a marvelous job of playing the Gestapo role.

He threatened me with several citations and said my "mistake" would cost me dearly. I told him shooting the deer was no mistake and that he should do what he felt he had to do. I would take my lumps and write my weekly column about the experience in the Janesville Gazette.

After a little parlay the wardens confiscated the deer's rack and sent me on my way. Ridley cautioned "I'll be watching you!" I replied "I'll be watching you too, Boyt. Don't forget that!"

I know that if the Old Guy and Sprink were still alive they

16

would have been pleased.

My only other encounter with law enforcement was a few years back on the Illinois River. It was a tough bite that cold early March day. I kept just two walleyes, a 20 incher and another fish about 16 inches long. Fourteen inches was the keeper size at that time.

I was in the process of preparing my rig for the drive home, still wearing a PFD. There were additional PFD's on the back of all four seats of my deep vee walleye boat. Probably adequate floation for somebody who was fishing solo.

The young warden approached with his hand on his gun, asking to see my license. I don't remember his name, but "Fife" still comes to mind. This star packer was not comfortable with his authority, feeling compelled to throw his weight around.

He asked if I had any fish. I directed him to the two walleyes swimming in the livewell. He grabbed the shorter of the two, using a 40 inch ruler in the boat to check it for legality. The walleye passed muster with two inches to spare.

He then grabbed the bigger fish and held it up to the tape. My circuit breaker popped. "Don't you think if the short fish was legal that the longer fish would be too?" I asked.

The warden stood there red faced. "Let me see your fire extinguisher and a whistle!" he barked. They were quickly produced.

"Where is your throwable PFD?" He asked. I smiled and told him it was still in my ice fishing tent. This was the first open water trip of the year and I had forgotten to put it in the boat.

"Aha! I gotcha!" he snorted.

"Yeah, you've got me," I replied. "Standing in a parking lot, wearing a PFD with four more life jackets within easy reach."

"The law says you have to have a throwable PFD," he growled back. I asked why, since I obviously had enough floatation to avoid drowning in a parking lot.

He said "so somebody can throw that cushion to you and save your life if you fall in the river."

Sarcasm reared its ugly head. "If I'm fishing alone and I fall in the river, who would crawl in my boat to throw me the PFD?" I wondered. This time the warden's circuit breaker popped. I was issued a warning ticket for failure to have a PFD in a parking lot.

About 15 years ago a guide who had a captain's license who worked on Lake Winnebago argued that anybody guiding these waters should have a captain's license because Winnebago was big and dangerous water, just like the Great Lakes where a captain's license is required to operate a sport fishing charter.

Of course the government jumped at the chance to rein in freedom and charge money for the privilege in the process. A law was passed requiring anybody operating a boat for hire on navigable waters to hold a valid USCG captain's license.

In Wisconsin this includes the Rock River clear up to the point where it starts near Horicon Marsh. The water here is three feet wide and ankle deep. Waters downstream from the Sac dam on the Wisconsin River are also deemed navigable, even though Wisconsin's namesake river flows over 200 miles before it reaches the Sac dam. Those who guide from this point upstream are exempt from the USCG license requirement.

The next dam upstream is at the beautiful Wisconsin Dells, where taking in the scenery from the famous Wisconsin Ducks has been a tourist attraction for decades.

These military surplus amphibious vehicles carry about 20 passengers who are treated to narration about the beautiful Dells by a pimple-faced college kid not required to have a captain's license.

Is this a case of absent common sense or politics as usual? I'll report. You decide.

The paper chase to obtain the Operator of Uninspected Passenger Vessel license is beyond unbelievable. It takes several months to gather all the documentation, including sea service logs, letters of recommendation, a social security card, certified copy of your birth certificate — the original with my little footprints which was issued from a hospital that later burned down was not good enough.

The applicant has to submit proof of good health, hearing, vision and be of both good moral character and clean urine. Producing the broomstick of the wicked witch of the west has been waived on those requesting licensure for a vessel displacing less than 99 tons.

Once all of the paperwork has been submitted and approved by a person who has had both their common sense gene and humor genes removed, the applicant is allowed to take a 40 hour course which makes it easier to pass the certified exam.

If you've never been convicted of more than a minor traffic violation and have about $1,000 to cover expenses all you have to do is pass two tests to take people out after bullheads on the Mississippi River.

At least this is the way it used to be. The last time I was up for the five year recertification the government added the prerequisite of a TWIC card before an applicant can even apply to jump through all of the other documentation hoops.

The Transportation Worker Identification Credential is a plastic card with all of the applicant's information hiding in a bar code. It even has biometric fingerprints in case you even get a cameo role on NCIS or CSI. All the government has to do is run your prints through their space age scanner and they will know that you are indeed you almost instantly.

All you have to do to get a TWIC card is take your valid captain's license, a pile of documentation and a check for $135 to the local TWIC office. Two weeks later those who pass muster can return to the TWIC office, place their thumb on the biometric fingerprint reader and pick up their new TWIC card.

The nearest TWIC facility to my hilltop redoubt is in Minneapolis 146 miles away. Two trips. Two days spent travelling. Just to pre-apply to renew a bullhead chasing permit.

The best part is, I have never been checked by the Coast Guard for my license. Another captain who runs a fishing float gets checked every year due to the nature of his operation. The last time they checked him he insisted the USCG run his TWIC card through their fancy scanner saying he just wanted to see how it worked.

He was told that this particular USCG unit didn't have one of the fancy scanners.

Somalia looks better every day.

"It turned out to be a good day on the river."

Have you got beers?

Most guide jobs start with a phone call or an email. Ron's first contact was by phone about 10 seconds after an entire tray full of beads, spinner blades and hooks splattered all over the den floor.

The den is a man cave, from Mossy Oak carpet on the floor to exposed ceiling joists for the living room above. Someday I'll hang a suspended ceiling. This project keeps getting kicked down the 'to do' list—like just about everything else not directly related to hunting or fishing.

Starting on this book has been a project swimming around the bottom of the bucket for years. It finally got started with a brutal arctic high pressure system squatting over northeast Iowa on an exceptionally cold late December morning.

Deer would be moving. But they would have to wait until evening. I woke up too late to get into the woods in a timely fashion. My wife said this day could start by scouring the kitchen sink which "still smells like fish." A half-dozen crappie scales do not deserve elaborate decontamination procedures.

Let me tell you about Ron's phone call. He asked if kids were welcome in my boat. I told him youngsters age 12-18 were more than welcome. In fact, I give a 10 percent discount to any client bringing a kid because the very future of sport fishing is at stake.

Ron said he had two boys, ages 8 and 12. Experience teaches considerable discretion is wise before inviting little humans just a few years removed from wetting their pants out on the Mississippi with anything more than frivolous delusions about catching fish.

"We've got a pond in the back yard, and young Stanley fishes almost every day," Ron assured me. His older brother, Glenn, is almost as good as I am."

Two red flags snapped up like passage of a gang of walleyes cruising through tip-ups at dusk. But these were the kind of flags which make you want to run like a scalded dog in the opposite direction.

You've gotta wonder about any parent who would refer to his eight-year-old son as 'Stanley' –and any adult who compares his angling expertise to a 12 year old and believes it to be a mark of achievement.

I looked at the beads and blades scattered across the Mossy

Oak carpet. The #4 hooks were a little tougher to see. At least a couple would eventually be found with bare feet, probably in the dark.

We agreed to meet at the Genoa boat launch a few days later. Ron whipped into the parking lot in a big Suburban with a huge fish-and-ski boat in tow. I thought it was some city boy about to ask directions. This rig certainly didn't look like conveyance for a Dad with two eager young fishermen.

Two men occupied the front seats of the Truckster, with almost a basketball team of youngsters howling and bouncing in the back seats.

"Are you Cap'n. Ted?" the driver grinned "This is my buddy, Roman. We're here to go fishin'!"

I reminded the beaming man of our phone conversation about a trip with a man and two kids. Although my captain's license allows taking up to six souls out on the Mississippi, three anglers is all I'll take in my 19 foot Lund Alaskan. This guideline is based on mathematical logic, to wit: O'Brien's Corollary.

O'Brien's Corollary is derived from Murphy's Law which states "if anything can go wrong, it will." O'Brien and Murphy were lifelong friends. His summation of Murphy's profundity is accurate, "My old pal Murphy is an optimist."

Plugging in the numbers: take three six-foot rods with about one foot of line undulating from the tip. Add a crankbait with two treble hooks to the end of each line, factoring in at least two of the wands are in the hands of folks who probably haven't been stung by hooks before.

March this crew into a 19 foot boat and park the boat just downstream from a school of magnum white bass on a feeding rip and you might ponder how many times Murphy hooked O'Brien before they finally quit fishing together.

I tried to be cordial and diplomatic when explaining this recipe for disaster to my potential client. Thankfully, he understood.

"How 'bout you take three of the kids? Ron offered. "Glenn can jump in the boat with us and we'll follow you!"

I wished I was home doing cartwheels across the den floor in the dark. A pragmatic response from the perspective of a weathered merchant marine captain was called for.

"Ron, the Mississippi River is a beautiful but deceptively dangerous place. I can't be responsible for watching three kids out there, let alone trying to teach three kids to fish. The ratio must be no more than one child per adult, and I've got to tell you that if you want me to babysit it will be much tougher to put you on fish and be successful."

"You're absolutely correct, Captain...how 'bout you take the two eight-year-olds and my buddy, Roman. He hasn't fished much, but he's a sharp guy. Roman is from Lithuania. He's only been in this country a little over a year. I'll follow you in my boat with Glenn and Vlad."

Looking back, I think Ron had envisioned this scenario all along. He's from the Chicago area. Folks who live in urban environments tend to look at life like they are playing a role from the TV show Survivor, which has the motto 'Outlive, Outlast, Outplay'.

Maybe perpetual scheming is a necessary survival skill for city folks. It always seems like they are trying to play you for some unseen advantage, negotiating deals in every interaction where one party must win and it will never be you unless you take part in the game.

I've never been wired that way, one reason why I moved to northeast Iowa. Folks here are for the most part straightforward and genuine, just like the River and the bluffs which watch her pass.

Northeast Iowa has some jerks which would score right off the charts even in a jungle like Chicago. Their number is few, with reputations that are usually regional rather than local.

The polite term for these folks is "stinkers". When forced to deal with one of them you do your best to be cordial, but the antennae go up before a word is said or given. With most other northeast Iowans there is no white lie window dressing. If we say yes, we mean yes. If we say no, we mean no. But if there is any way we can help you out we certainly will.

This is a tough and unforgiving place to live, with no need or inclination to be ostentatious. If you need a new truck, you buy a new truck. Work trucks with vinyl floors and roll-up windows are in high demand. You won't see one in the used aisle of a local car dealer for very long.

The millionaire farmer who owns the bottomland below my house and the woods up the bluff behind it drives around in a battered blue S-10 pickup truck with a feedbag stuffed in the right front quarter panel which rust has pretty much eaten away. Even the bag is a tribute to necessity. All the roads are gravel here. The bag helps keep the dust out in the summer and snow out in the winter.

I told Ron to launch his boat and park his rig next to my GMC work truck and invited Roman, Stanley and Roman's quiet little daughter Rema into the boat for the standard USCG briefing while we waited for Ron so we could get underway.

Roman stood silent while I fitted the kids with life jackets and

25

reviewed emergency procedures.

"Here is the USCG required fire extinguisher," I nodded toward the steering console while securing Stanley's PFD. "In the event of a fire, follow me. I will already be in the River."

This comment usually generates a chuckle or at least a friendly smirk from new clients. Roman stood stone faced, perhaps a little concerned.

"Are we good to go, Roman" I asked.

"You got beers? "He blurted in a thick Lithuanian accent.

"No, no beers, Roman," I said "The captain isn't allowed to have any alcohol, just like on a commercial airliner. But feel free to bring a couple of beers if you want. You're an adult."

"No beers?" he asked, a little more agitated.

"No beers for me," I repeated, starting to feel like comedian Bob Newhart doing his famous telephone routine.

"No beers!" Roman growled, putting up his dukes and stepping in my direction. I responded with a similar posture, not quite knowing what to make of the situation. Roman growled "No beers!" again in his thick Lithuanian accent, punching at the air between us. His attempts at communication finally succeeded, forcing a burst of spontaneous laughter.

"Oh, you mean bears!" I snorted. "We see black bears around here every now and then. But they are never a problem. By this time Ron was in his young ship of a semi-fishing boat ready to go.

I gave silent thanks that this was only going to be a half-day trip, opting to go after the always willing largemouth bass. Stanley had his own rod. It was a St. Croix with a decent spinning reel. Maybe this kid did know how to fish. Maybe his Dad was simply flush with money and saw nothing wrong with putting a hundred dollar outfit in the hands of an eight-year old.

I swapped his deep-diving crankbait for a white dot Black Fury Mepps spinner and handed Roman and Rema a couple of my rods which were already set up with Chompers Salty Sinker senko-style worms, rigged wacky style.

By the efficient way Ron launched his boat, it appeared he might know at least a little bit about fishing. On some subliminal level I must have fallen into the urban status quo of gamesmanship. "You might try a chrome/blue Rat-L-Trap or maybe a white spinnerbait," I shouted back to him. "We're going to work down along this rocky shoreline and see if any bass are home."

Trying to put three novices on fish is a full plate for any guide. I charge an additional $75 for a third angler, which pretty much cancels out the 10 percent discount for bringing a kid along.

I figured Ron would see how hard you had to work to ensure kids had a memorable time and might tip accordingly. This is the way we do business over on the River. If urban gamesmanship had him thinking that the base guide's rate and no gratuity was the way to go I would know in four hours.

It turned out to be a great day on the River. Bass were eager to bite. My crew caught a couple of crappies, pike, smallmouth and white bass in between tangling with the largemouths. From the commotion and occasional squeal in the boat which followed us it seemed like Ron and his kids were having a good trip, too.

Rema was a sweet little girl, almost too serious for an eight-year-old. She caught her share of fish with little more than a wry smile when I netted them showing considerable fanfare to generate excitement.

Her cool efficiency provided a sense of understanding about how some of Russia's most efficient snipers during World War II were female.

I don't know if Stanley was hyperactive or merely fed a diet of Red Bull and Snickers bars. It's been decades since my kids were eight years old. He was probably just being a typical kid, more enthralled by turtles on logs, eagles gliding overhead and other frenetic tangents than focusing on fishing. We could all benefit from his perspective on life.

He fished a little, too. But had to be reminded on more than one occasion that the landing net was for scooping fish and not swinging at butterflies. Roman doted on his daughter and pretty much tried to tune Stanley's antics out.

He obviously enjoyed seeing his daughter catch her first fish, reveling in the joy of being a parent for the most part rather than fishing on his own.

We were almost back at the boat ramp when Roman picked up a rod again. There is a small pool at the Genoa boat ramp with quiet water which often holds fish. Most folks overlook this obvious spot, hell-bent to take a boat ride looking for greener pastures.

Stanley cast his Mepps spinner towards a rocky outcropping at the leading edge of the pool.

Roman announced "I cast here," and let one fly from the back of the boat. Unfortunately, he forgot to hang on to my $150 rod. The rod and lure promptly sank in about four feet of water. Line in between still floated on the surface. I thought there might be a chance of getting this gear back if we moved quickly.

This endeavor was put on hold when squeals erupted from the

bow of the boat. A fat 36 inch pike had garwoofled Stanley's lure and didn't want to give it back. The boy was so stunned by this assault that he forgot what the crank on the reel was for and ran toward the back of the boat.

Frequent thoughts that this had been a challenging day developed deeper meaning with Roman, Rema and the landing net now standing between Stanley and his tormentor.

Somehow I managed to lift the line and grab the net without allowing any slack. Ron saw all the commotion and was busy snapping photos of the entire clown act — including a great shot of Stanley beaming with pride as I lifted the big pike over the gunwale.

This may have been the motivation behind Ron's generous tip. I was thankful but certainly glad to get off the water that day. Looking back, this adventure always makes me smile.

Ron still books trips with me several times each year. Somehow, he and the boys always seem to catch fish even under the most obscene conditions.

Fishing guides quickly learn the wisdom of quietly accepting the praise when clients find success on those days when you think the bite is going to be tough. Catching is part of the fishing experience. But it's only one wrinkle in the grand adventure.

"Being a dad is the most important job you'll ever have."

Guiding

The Wisconsin Dept. of Natural Resources is this state's greatest foil for everyone interested in the outdoors who is not employed by the WDNR. Working as a newspaper columnist since 1973, the WDNR has provided endless fodder for my outdoor columns in several daily newspapers.

No matter what this agency does, some segment of the population which enjoys the outdoors resource will be somewhere between displeased and snot-slinging, howling mad.

Like most states, Wisconsin has a portion of their sprawling bureaucracy dedicated to regulation of fishing guides. Unlike Illinois and Iowa which essentially license a boat, Wisconsin licenses the person operating the boat.

This guide license costs Wisconsin residents $40 and non-residents $100 for a 3 x 9 inch piece of paper which authorizes the bearer to "guide, direct, or assist other persons in fishing..." It says absolutely nothing about the guide actually doing the fishing when engaged in the profession of guiding.

I seldom fish with persons who are paying me to guide them, for several solid reasons. First, if I'm fishing the connection between my mind, body and the hook somewhere out there in the big River is my primary focus.

When I actually fish it is in the role of alpha predator. You seldom see a fat coyote that is preoccupied with a monarch butterfly while on a mission to catch a rabbit. Focus is a major key to being a consistently successful fisherman.

Following this pursuit on the Mississippi usually involves boat control as well. Boat control on a river is much more difficult than keeping a watercraft in the optimum orientation to pull fish out of a lake.

Rivers have currents. Currents can quickly push a boat into obstructions and other potentially dangerous situations. Good fishermen adopt the sniper credo "one shot-one kill".

Every single cast should be made with the anticipation of a five pound smallmouth or walleye waiting for your hook to come seductively past her face. Every single cast.

When you're fishing this means positioning the boat to allow the perfect cast every time. If the guide is fishing his clients are at the very least slightly out of position to make that perfect cast. This alone increases the odds that their hook will find a fish.

It is usually possible to position the boat so that two anglers can offer their bait in an optimum presentation. But with three lines in the water the difficulty in setting everybody up to kick a finned field goal increases geometrically. This is why I charge extra for more than two anglers in the boat and seldom pick up a rod when three persons are my responsibility.

O'Leary's theorem of Murphy's Law kicks in when a guide's line is in the water.

Essentially this observation says if a 10 pound walleye is in the vicinity it will find the guide's hook instead of the clients.

It is a rare client indeed who would relish the concept of paying a base rate of $40 per hour to watch me catch the fish he has been dreaming about.

There are some clients who show up alone insisting on a gunfight between themselves and the guide in a contest to see who the better angler is. With a very few exceptions in my boat the client will always leave the water believing he has opened a can of whoopass and sprayed me down with the contents.

Sometimes this "fishing lesson" comes with sincere advice on how to improve my game. It is often accompanied by a substantial gratuity for which I am forever grateful.

Ego can be fatal for a fishing guide-- at least ego worn on the sleeve of a fashionably frayed flannel shirt.

A client who really wants to engage a guide in a fishing competition on the guide's home waters is usually hoping to fulfill some kind of angling fantasy where the client is the dominant pro.

According to the designation on my Wisconsin guide's license I am supposed to "...assist other persons in fishing..." If this is some variation of a Kevin VanDam pipe dream, call me your dream weaver.

To use football analogies a good guide is an offensive lineman, a long snapper or at best the guy who sets the ball on the tee just right so the place kicker can score the winning goal with no time left on the clock.

In military terms a good guide is a sergeant who makes every effort to see that a green lieutenant or ensign has the command presence of a staff officer. A good guide is the foreman who does everything in his power to allow talented artisans which report to him the freedom to work their trade without being told how to do it. He is a supporting actor or a stuntman, but never the star.

Those in this role have the power to make the "star" look very good or at the very least inept. There is considerable art in following either course without the person paying the freight realizing he is not the puppet master.

A guide's best tool in this endeavor is his boat. Precise boat control is often difficult on the Mississippi, especially with a strong south wind and River levels far above normal pool.

If you can keep the boat in the optimum orientation for fishing while having the client believe you're just kicking back enjoying their company and those spectacular vistas the River always provides, you are working like the pro you are supposed to be.

This is a position of considerable power during the time clients share your boat. I must admit abusing it just a little bit with clients who need their ears pinned back. The degree to which I try to influence difficulty is driven by my perception of the client's attitude.

Our actual ability as fishermen is limited to basic tasks like tying on a hook. Even this basic operation is difficult for those who lack good vision and dexterity. I believe we can try our very best, but every fish is a gift from God!

I will do everything possible for folks with the general attitude they are merely players in the grand scheme. Others who believe they are the best fishermen who ever lived get a little less help.

Fishing is a microcosm of life. We go through stages of growth as human beings. We also have the opportunity to grow as anglers. A guide has the potential to influence this process.

"Darrin is one squared away young man."

My nephew Darrin is a case in point. It was obvious since this young man was stumbling around in diapers that he had a fire in his belly to be a competent outdoorsman.

Words can't express my profound joy in young Darrin harvesting his first trophy buck, first pheasant and first turkey.

There is a story within a story about the kid's first Tom. His mom let him skip school that warm April morning. I could hear Darrin chuckling to himself as we heard the bus carrying his brother drive past the woodlot where we were set up –just as the gobbler started sneaking up through the briar bushes amongst the towering oaks.

I could see his hands shaking and his skinny back heaving with hyperventilation as the 23 pound longbeard tracked ever closer. At a range of 25 yards I whispered "shoot".

Nothing is louder than a 12 gauge shotgun breaking the silence of April woods in the morning or the flapping of turkey wings after a well placed head shot. I made him carry the big bird back to the truck a half-mile away.

Since it was too late to go to school we headed for Apple Canyon Lake about seven miles from his Dad's northwest Illinois farm. The water temperature was only 45 degrees back in bays with northern exposures. Conventional wisdom says this warmest available water should hold the best chances at finding active bass.

Darrin caught several fish on a Rat-L-Trap lipless vibrating crankbait from Apple Canyon's ultra-clear waters. Then he let out a squeal which had me wondering if I had a niece or a nephew in the back of the boat.

"Uncle, Ted! A MUSKIE!" he blurted in half the time it took you to read those words. Sure enough, a mid 40-inch toother was sunning itself in about six feet of water.

Springtime muskies engaged in this pursuit seldom feel like chasing lures.

I put a huge tube jig on an always ready muskie rod and told Darrin to cast about three feet in front of the muskie's nose. On the fourth cast the big fish glided forward and slurped up the tube jig.

Darrin set the hook and pandemonium ensued until I slid the net under this beautiful silvery green creature five minutes later. She was just over 43 inches long.

The odds of a person shooting their first gobbler and catching their first muskie in the same day are right off the charts. My only regret that day was not buying a lottery ticket for the kid.

I sent photos of the fish and turkey along with a little write up to several local papers. They jumped on the story. Young Darrin Marcure was a celebrity, with a real opportunity to believe he had considerably more outdoor skill than was actually the case.

Two years later Darrin was developing quite well as a fisherman when he reached a critical point in the journey. We were fishing Apple Canyon again and I was doing my darnedest to orient the boat to give him the best shot at the fish.

I wasn't keeping score when he announced he had me down something like 13 bass to 4. Then he announced "I am probably one of the top 10 tube jig fishermen in Illinois". My eyes must have twinkled. I know my smile stretched from ear to ear.

Without his knowledge the orientation of the boat changed just a little bit as we worked along the shoreline. At the end of the day he was still keeping score. The numbers were something like 41 to 15. Darrin got to use the net a lot.

"So tell me what it's like to be one of the top 10 tube jig fishermen in the state," I chuckled.

Darrin looked at his feet for a few seconds before looking me in the eye. "I guess I've got a lot to learn, "he said, shaking his head. My smile was like an echo—it came right back.

On a chilly November morning back in 2010 Darrin called, breathing heavily. Initially, I thought he was in trouble.

"Thirteen points!" he blurted "Thirteen points! Huge! Huge! Huge!" After a brief conversation in which Darrin was mostly speaking in tongues he agreed to send digital photos of his trophy buck as soon as possible.

My biggest deer to date is a 10 pointer scoring 174 inches which hangs in a place of honor on the living room wall. Darrin's buck is bigger. A mentoring uncle could not possibly have more pride. The Bean and Darrin's Dad did a marvelous job of guiding Darrin toward manhood.

He's been on his own since high school. By age 22 he was running his own construction business. Darrin learned early on in life that there is no place for excuses. He has always accepted responsibility and consequences for his actions. This is one squared away young man.

This life lesson comes a little harder to others. Sometimes they don't get there at all, or if they do the epiphany didn't come while fishing from my boat. Such is the case with Dr. Willis, an anesthesiologist who believed he was also the Doctor of Fish.

Dr. Willis hired me on several occasions, bringing his long suffering wife Ellen along to bear witness of his self professed angling excellence. Repeat clients are usually a source of great fulfillment for a guide. Their return is validation that his work is appreciated. It is also accompanied with a level of chemistry which can morph from guide/client to the point where you're fishing buddies having a whale of a good time.

This was not the case with Willis, who tried to pervert our outings in a strange adolescent attempt to show his wife that he was a better fisherman than I was. Men tend to be competitive by nature. Testosterone can drive the male of the species to accomplish Herculean tasks. It can also push a cautious savvy buck into the path of a fatal arrow.

Ellen was an attractive woman who was clearly not attracted to the hubris of her husband. I believe it was a combination of empathy for Ellen and male tendencies to compete for the attention of a good looking female that pushed me into the delicate ballet of making her husband look good while attempting to goad him into facing the reality that he was a pathetic poseur.

The doctor insisted that I fish with them. I made sure that he always caught more and bigger fish than I did, while doing my best to help his wife catch enough fish to euchre the little tyrant from crowing that he should be immortalized in statue at the Freshwater Fishing Hall of Fame in Hayward, Wisconsin.

It wasn't chemistry which led the doctor to book multiple trips with me. I believe it was a combination of ego, vindication and manifestation of the little man complex in an attempt to bully others thus reinforcing a delusion of superiority. I'm no psychologist. I'm just a fishing guide. From this vantage point I can only offer this opinion: Dr. Willis was a jerk.

The only thing a person can truly control in dealing with a jerk is attitude. It would be easy to lapse into metaphysical lament wondering "Why, oh why God did you put so many jerks on the planet at the same time?" A better man would be truly professional and simply try to provide the best guide service possible.

I tried this tactic for awhile, feeling considerable angst every time I threw a wad of Dr. Willis' twenties into the cookie jar.

Finally the inevitable Day of Reckoning arrived. Dr. Willis showed up in his black BMW with Ellen in tow, a brand new GLoomis GLX SJR 781 rod, top-of-the-line reel and a plastic bag containing his

38

"secret weapon".

Red flags should go up any time somebody shows up professing expertise and toting brand new gear.

I remember going on an outdoor writer junket to a hunt club one time with several accomplished communicators. Many outdoor writers have trouble loading a pump shotgun or pull starting an outboard motor, merely cloaking themselves in expertise by chronicling the accomplishments of others who can really walk their talk.

Most of the time I would rather be called a liberal Democrat than an outdoors writer, although I must admit playing the writer card on more than one occasion in return for consideration on goods and services.

I was wearing the same old tan hunting coat which had covered my back five days a week all season long for years. My Cabela's Goretex bib overalls were only a couple months old but had been worn essentially every day on the water or in the field. We were headed out after pheasants which had been rocked to sleep before being placed a couple hundred yards in front of a knee high chicken wire fence in a field of standing corn.

As we rode on benches in the back of a pickup truck to partake in this "hunt" a well known writer from suburban Chicago sporting new Abercrombie & Fitch upland attire and a little hat with a feather in it felt compelled to comment on my pants.

"How old are those drawers, Peck?" he snipped. I looked down at the dried blood of at least three deer, multiple ducks, pheasants and tears from stumbling through heavy brush and growled back "About two months, Mike." All others foregathered did not need to be told there was a hunter in the house.

Back to Willis who produced a brand new shrink wrapped, hard plastic display case full of Banjo Minnows which he had no doubt purchased for the outrageous sum of $19.95 after viewing an infomercial promising More Fish-Bigger Fish.

"I'm gonna kick your ass today!" he announced in no uncertain terms. We had clearly reached the tipping point.

"Doc, those baits may work but you can catch just as many fish throwing a tube jig rigged backwards for a mere nickel per lure," I shot back.

"We'll see about that!" he crowed.

I was not about to enter into a competition with some clueless clown who thought he could bring a box cutter to a gun fight in the sincere belief that he would come away victorious.

If there was going to be any ass displacement on this trip, it would be from me handing the doctor's own posterior back to him with no apologies.

The issue thus joined, I set Ellen up with a tube jig rigged backwards and we proceeded down the shoreline in a contest to finesse some bass.

I wasn't about to tell the doctor he was using the wrong color or working his lure too fast. Instead I concentrated on keeping the boat in an orientation where Ellen had the best advantage while coaxing her in catching fish.

At day's end Ellen was bubbling about the best fishing trip of her life. Dr. Willis wrote out a check for the exact amount of the trip, and then pushed his selection of Banjo Minnows into my hands growling "here's your tip". I never heard from him again.

Snapshots

A day on the Mississippi is like turning the crank on a jack-in-the-box. This toy is not to be confused with an X-Box or a Wii. If the Chinese ever shoot down our communications satellites electronics will be useless and those who survive will once again be content by turning a crank and watching a clown pop up when least expected.

Brandon Maxwell experienced a spontaneous brain freeze one sultry August day several years ago when a nine-pound bowfin—a.k.a. dogfish—slurped in a tiny piece of nightcrawler intended for a bluegill.

Dogfish can be traced back to Jurassic times, with a crude lung that allows them to gulp in oxygen. This is a handy trait in low oxygen environments. Dogfish have an evil, serpent-like snout with a mouthful of razor sharp teeth. Their dorsal fin runs clear back to a squared off tail, resulting in tremendous power when trying to escape something like a fish hook.

Maxwell was a skinny little guy with nervous habits. He could have easily filled in for Don Knotts in the role of Barney Fife on the old Andy Griffith show. He was a chain smoker with an annoying habit of drumming his fingers on the gunnel of the boat while waiting for his pencil floats to dance away in tow from a scrappy bluegill.

More than once I thought about suggesting we tie on buzz-baits to cast for bass. Sultry August days are ideal for this kind of pursuit. But Maxwell wanted bluegills and we were anchored up near a substantial school of them around a fallen tree down in the Winneshiek slough.

Brandon Maxwell was a mechanic by trade. Guides like taking blue collar folks fishing more than executives, doctors or lawyers. Most folks who work in suits tend to have more money than sense and little concept of tipping for a job well done.

Executives are tolerable, especially when they are on a corporate trip with clients, paying with a corporate check and a built-in gratuity. Often an executive will treat a client he is trying to woo with a fishing trip, with knowledge that this companion likes to fish.

This can be a good thing if the client of my client realizes that listening to the guide will usually result in more fish. It is a bad thing if the would be mark thinks he could teach bass pro Kevin VanDam a thing or two.

Some doctors and lawyers are excellent fishermen, with the resources for fishing the best waters with the best guides. They tend to be pretty sharp folks, picking up at least the concepts of fishing quickly.

Doctors and lawyers are also terrible tippers, at least most who have M.D. or J.D. after their name. One exception is the Johnson brothers—a doctor and a lawyer. One brother lives in Chicago, the other in Milwaukee.

The Old Guy used to say there are two things man can't create—land and time. God made only so much land. Many farmers are land rich and cash poor. But they get to spend every day out there working the land, resulting in a bond not unlike a River Rat feels for the River.

One Johnson brother purchased a beautiful tract of land near DeSoto on the Wisconsin side of the River. He has only walked this property a couple of times, never having the luxury to saunter through the woods in search of morels or shed antlers. Money is of little value if it can't buy the time to enjoy the wonders of nature.

These brothers are in their mid-30's. Until the winter of 2011 they had never been ice fishing, although both reported viewing countless DVD's and reading many articles on the hardwater experience.

A break in the ominous clouds of scheduling opened a brief window in late January. Doctor Todd called and wondered if I could find time for a half-day trip the following afternoon.

Normally, I would turn down such a request. But there was need to get out on the ice anyway, as another trip was on the books just a day after the Johnsons wanted to go and I needed to go find some active fish.

It took these gentlemen little time to understand the basics of electronics and bait presentation. There were fish under almost every one of the dozen holes I poked through 25 inches of ice, but most were less than eager due to passage of a substantial cold front.

It was all they could do to put enough bluegills on the ice for a good meal. But they were grateful for the experience and a chance to forget about work for awhile. Dr. Todd shoved a wad of bills into my almost frozen mitt. I didn't take time to count the money until arriving home. They gave me a $137 tip for a four hour trip!

Fortunately, Johnson is a common name. There is little chance that other doctors and lawyers who like to fish will be able to seek out the Johnson brothers and insist on some kind of sanction for unsolicited benevolence.

Doctors and lawyers are still in a dead-heat tie for flagrant frugality in the gratuity department, second only to ministers, pastors, rabbis and priests. Some ministers are paid little more than starvation wages. A few are well compensated for their efforts.

When Jesus was in the process of rounding up his disciples, his first recruits were Andrew and Simon Peter. A little farther down the shore Jesus saw another pair of fishing brothers, James and John who were fishing with their Dad, Zebedee.

All these guys immediately knew Jesus was the Son of God and dropped everything to follow him. God always provided, just like He said He would. On one of their treks Peter was asked if Jesus planned on paying a "temple tax". Peter was somewhat frantic, because he had no money.

Jesus knew all about the circumstances before Peter even got home to ask the Lord what they were going to do. In Matthew 17 Jesus

44

showed he was the ultimate fishing guide by telling Peter where to cast and solve their cash flow situation.

In another Bible story Jesus was on the beach cooking breakfast for his fishin' buddies. There were no bag limits back then. Had this been the case and the shore lunch was in Wisconsin Jesus' fateful day in court would have come a little earlier in the gospels.

Continuing on this digression, ministers have been called to follow Christ perpetually reassured that God will provide. I have always wondered who picks up the check when four pastors meet for lunch. Probably a toss up between the restaurant owner and his chef.

I identify with Peter more than any of the other original disciples. I fish for a living, but don't charge men of the cloth because they have a tougher job than anyone else on the planet. Some who try to follow Christ's teachings remember that four of his first fishers of men were pulling nets because they were pretty short of drachmas to begin with.

I give a 10 percent discount to any client who brings a kid, police, fire, EMS and military. Preachers can fish for free. I tell them how much it costs me to launch the boat—about fifty bucks a day when you figure in license fees, insurance, gas, wear and tear on gear and a couple of other variables

Sometimes I come off the water $50 in the hole. Sometimes I break even. Sometimes I make a little money. None of this matters, because it's all God's money, anyway.

Everybody who jumps in my guide boat is there for recreation. There are only two essential rules: leave all your demons and your Game Boy at the dock. Doctors and lawyers aren't thinking of surgery or litigation if I'm doing my job. Tips are not required, but certainly appreciated. Tips are usually $20-$100.

When a doctor or lawyer tips me a shiny new Roosevelt dime, I know it has gained numismatic luster from the bottom of a pocket in a Brooks Brothers suit.

Working men are the best tippers. When Maxwell got out of the boat at day's end he apologized for only offering a $20 tip because he had to purchase a new pair of pliers.

I should have tipped him twenty bucks for entertainment which occurred about midway through our half-day excursion.

Brandon was sitting in the bow of the boat, puffing and drumming away with eyes darting between the three pencil floats which we hoped would bounce with fleeing fish.

Suddenly one of the bobbers was gone an about to take the 10 foot Crappie Commander rod with it. Dogfish are a worthy adversary with baitcast gear. When you try to tussle with them using what amounts to a flyrod with a spinning reel taped to it you have your hands full.

It took Maxwell a good 15 minutes to bring this angry dogfish to the landing net. A bluegill sent one of the other bobbers skittering away. Brandon told me to catch that fish while he removed the hook from the dogfish.

With hands trembling more than usual, fired up by epinephrine and endorphins Brandon Maxwell used his stainless steel, needle-nosed SnapOn pliers to remove the hook from this hefty prehistoric beast.

He looked at the fish. Then he looked at the pliers. Back to the fish. Back to the pliers. Sensory overload from combat resulted in temporary brain freeze. He threw the pliers in the River!

46

My first cascade of laughter went into overdrive as he scowled at the dogfish and then whined "Those were fifty dollar pliers!"

* * *

Back in May of 2010 a man phoned wondering if I would mind guiding an elderly woman. He said he would be coming along to ensure she wouldn't be too much of a burden.

Marge was in her late 70's, frail and somewhat stoop-shouldered from a hard life which included raising six kids after being widowed.

The kids decided to give her a fishing trip as a Mother's Day gift. Roger, the youngest son, had drawn the short straw and was tasked with delivering the gift.

There was something about Marge's eyes which told me this fishing trip was not her first rodeo. I had rods rigged up for both catfish and panfish, two pursuits which are practically a sure thing and not labor intensive on the grand Mississippi River.

Marge wanted to fish bass. Smallmouth bass if we could find them. By late May both largemouth and smallmouth bass are done spawning. Largemouth were settling into a lazy pattern relating to wood and developing weed growth back in the sloughs, with smallmouth generally mad at the world and taking it out on anything foolish enough to swim close along rocks where there was a little current.

Roger was a decent fisherman, taught rudimentary casting skills by his mother before his interests strayed away from the water. It was clear Marge knew how to handle a spinning rod. Every cast she made landed lightly and right where it was supposed to go.

I had them start out throwing Chompers Salty Sinkers, a salt laden plastic worm which waffles seductively through the water column when rigged "wacky style" with a #4 Circle hook impaled through its middle.

Patience is the key when fishing wacky-rigged Senko style baits with a circle hook. If you try to stick the fish when it first picks up the lure, you'll miss them every time. Wait until the fish tries to take the rod out of your hand and respond with a slow sweep in the opposite direction and you'll hook about 90 percent of the fish in the corner of the mouth.

Roger and his Mom had caught probably 20 bass using this method, with the feisty grandma accounting for three fourths of the catch. We kept seeing the swirl of a big bass blowing up on minnows atop rocks in very shallow water.

Marge wanted to catch this fish. I tied a frog pattern Smithwick Devil's Horse on another rod, instructing Marge to cast where the fish had just surfaced. It took probably 10 casts before this 19 ½ inch smallmouth could no longer resist.

When a whopper smallmouth eats a surface bait in shallow water it will almost always rocket skyward. This one fit the typical profile, and then proceeded to cartwheel across the surface shaking its head.

Marge held on for dear life, fighting the biggest bass she had ever seen. Five minutes later the smallie was in the net and this gritty fisherwoman collapsed on a boat seat with an ear to ear grin.

She wanted to release the fish after we took some pictures, but asked me to put it in the livewell for a few minutes so she could recuperate.

"I'm ready now," she chirped. Please take close up pictures above the waist. I knew I should have worn my Depends!"

Roger was embarrassed. Marge had no shame. Those who live long enough accept the facts of life as they come, and savor every minute of it.

*　*　*

Mel is a young Christian counselor who grew up in Taiwan. His friend, Li, was from the northwest coming to the Mississippi with the dual mission of visiting Mel and doing research for her master's thesis on hydrology with plans on becoming an engineer.

Even though she was in her early 30's Li had never been fishing. Mel is an outstanding hunter, fisherman and frequent client living and working around Madison, Wisconsin.

It was early spring. The River was almost at flood stage, with water temperatures in the upper 40's and a cold front howling in overhead. Not exactly what you would call good fishing conditions.

Li was scheduled to fly back to Portland later that day, and told Mel she wanted to try fishing in the few hours free time before her plane left LaCrosse. Mel caught a nice pike and a decent walleye. Li had beginner's luck going for her and caught multiple species including a couple of bass.

Spring fishing is almost always a run-and-gun situation. Many promising spots will come up empty. When you find fish, they may be concentrated in a very small area.

Li put the hurt on a half dozen bass with just enough time to try one more spot before the trip was over.

When I fired up the big Evinrude a plastic spray bottle of fish attractant scent blew out of the boat. We spun back around and Mel fished it out of the River.

"What's that?" Li asked innocently. "Fish attractant scent, "I

49

replied. Mel's smirk told me further explanation was in order.

"What does this scent smell like," she wondered. The little devil which sometimes whispers in my right ear prompted a small deviation from pure professionalism.

"Jasmine!" I blurted. "It has the smell of sweet, sweet flowers. Fish simply can't resist it. Mel can tell you this jasmine fish attractant is one of my favorite secret weapons."

Mel had a little devil perched on his shoulder, too. "He's absolutely correct, Li," Mel chimed in "I'm surprised they don't market this stuff as perfume. Would you like Cap'n. Ted to put a little spritz on your wrist?"

With two substantial squirts of the oily stuff from the spray bottle Li was initiated into the fellowship of fishermen.

"Oh, Li! My mistake," I snorted. This is garlic spray. The jasmine must be in another compartment of the boat."

Mel later told me it took a very expensive dinner to make amends. I'm sure everybody on that commuter hop to Minneapolis left the plane thinking of spaghetti.

*   *   *

Fishermen have a reputation for not telling the truth. We are not born liars, but we certainly learn this dubious trait quicker than most folks. Lies may stem from feelings of inadequacy, prompted by a need to prove expertise in the eyes of peers.

Falsehoods may come trickling out because of guilt, driven by the notion that the prevaricator should have been engaged in something more productive than fishing. Motivation for a fisherman's lie seldom swells from malevolent intent. Rather, it is a survival skill, perhaps driven from fear—just like Peter denying Christ three times before the rooster crowed.

One of our biggest fears is that another fisherman will discover our secret honeyhole or little trick which gives the tiniest edge in friendly but unspoken competition out there on the water.

By hard work or good fortune we sometimes stumble across a little nugget. Sharing this discovery always has the potential for losing what you have found. Should this occur you have nobody to blame but yourself, because it was you who failed to judge a compatriot's intent or motivation.

A few years ago I made the mistake of taking Pastor Jim Ogden to a little spot on Pool 9 which was just a five minute walk from the highway. It was a great place to visit when time was short and the need to feel a solid tug on the line imperative to mental well being.

I didn't feel compelled to tell Pastor Jim to keep this place secret. This assumption is the kind of thing which goes unsaid between fishin' buddies. Unfortunately he never received instruction along these lines when growing up.

One balmy spring day I had an hour to kill on the way to an appointment in LaCrosse. Just enough time to catch a few white bass which often visit my once secret little spot.

The pastor's car was sitting in a little pull off area where I usually park. This didn't bother me. At least not much. When I saw the pastor, a guy from our church and his kid fishing the site of my frequent joy and catharsis and all three of them hooked up and laughing gleefully I felt betrayed. Pastor didn't know any better. Mea culpa.

When somebody pays you to guide them and you reveal little secrets it is understood that clients need not feel any guilt if they revisit the spot at a later date.

There is a small run of rip-rapped shoreline on a mid-stream island which attracts walleyes at spawning time around April 20 each year. A retired GM employee named Tom Mellencamp said he had been reading my stuff in the Janesville Gazette for years and wanted to see for himself if my words were fact-based or merely smoke.

You can't make a habit of telling blatant lies and survive as an outdoors writer or fishing guide for more than 30 years. But as my gut wrenching faux pas with Pastor Ogden reveals, there is often wisdom in revealing less than the truth in its entirety.

Mellencamp said he wanted to go after walleyes somewhere away from the dam, which attracts an unbelievable flotilla of boats in the spring. We eased up on my little walleye spot and this outstanding angler started pitching 1/8 ounce jigs with plastic tails right in the fish zone.

It didn't take long before his hook found a fish of substantial dimensions. Snickers of joy turned into growls of anguish when combat revealed a big carp rather than a heavy walleye at the end of my client's line.

Apparently the fire service isn't the only workplace where colorful language bursts forth during times of excitement or high stress. Mellencamp is the kind of person who feels compelled to keep his blue language skills well tinted in the course of casual conversation, ensuring his chosen adjectives will be both loud and fluent when the need arises.

The big carp triggered a substantial outburst and serious questions about my guiding abilities, when I suggested Tom try another cast. He became suddenly silent when another big fish slurped in the jig.

"It's probably another doggone carp!" he barked—or words to that effect, triggering further litany about my lack of guiding ability. The headshaking, bulldog fight this fish was engaged in had me wondering if Mellencamp had found the mother of all walleyes.

A couple minutes later a wide tail with a white spot on the bottom broke the surface of the River. It was immediately clear to both of us that he was battling a beaut.

She was 31 ¼ inches long. This fish was the biggest walleye of his life and the heaviest walleye to ever come in my boat on the Upper Mississippi River. My reward was a $100 tip.

The following summer gas prices were flirting with $4.00 per gallon. Casual boat rides were out of the question. I pulled into the ramp at Genoa and parked next to Mellencamp's rig—a candy apple red Suburban towing a candy apple red trailer for a Ranger 690 boat.

High water had me thinking fish might still be holding in a small pool near the ramp where they had been the night before. A number of folks recognize my Lund. Lots of boaters use that ramp. If they saw me catching fish, the glory days at this spot would be over.

I pulled the cowling off of my ever-faithful Evinrude to give casual observers the impression of motor trouble and launched the boat. Fish were stacked in there like I had never seen them before—walleyes, bass, pike…everything.

At least a dozen of them found freedom when given slack as a boater approached the ramp. Some folks offered assistance. I would just feign disgust and shake my head.

Suddenly Mellencamp came roaring up the River in his big Ranger, cussing all the way.

As he eased up to the ramp he cursed "Thirty-two gallons of

gas and I only caught four bass — and only two of them were legal. But at least I had a better day than you're having, Peck!"

I didn't have the heart to tell him I was having a very good day. For some obtuse reason I felt compelled to tweak ol' Tommy boy. It didn't take long to catch a couple of scrappy 16 inch smallmouth and put them in the livewell, with a plan for creating some kind of photo op to let my former client know the Mississippi was in a benevolent mood that day if you knew where to look.

Two teenage boys provided the opportunity. After they launched their beat up 16 foot Starcraft boat powered by an Elgin outboard I asked if they would hold my two smallmouth bass and let me take a quick picture.

This photo ran the following Sunday next to my column in the Janesville Gazette, clearly showing the Genoa boat ramp in the background. Tom Mellencamp phoned later that evening. If there is any college out there looking for somebody to teach a course entitled "Profanity as a second language" I know where they can find a suitable professor.

Men of the Cloth

The practice of guiding preachers for free dates back to my grandfather's day. My grand-dad Carlos "Cob" Robbe was a hard working carpenter back in the days before power tools were even dreamed of.

Cob was a craftsman, using his hands to create anything which needed to be created. One time he built a fishing rod combo out of a short 2 x 4 and some tin. This outfit brings new meaning to the term "meat pole".

The "reel" is a horizontal tin wheel about seven inches in diameter, somewhere within its inner workings are a couple of ball bearings which make this zero-ratio winch amazingly smooth given the materials Cob had to work with.

Grand-dad didn't get much time to fish back in the 1920s and 1930's, trying to raise six kids on a carpenter's wage. My mother was the youngest of the five girls. This designation provided the opportunity to sneak off with Cob on a Saturday afternoon if he wasn't doing some serious fishing with Rev. Seitner, pastor of the First Baptist Church in Mt. Carroll.

My Mom loved to fish almost as much as the Old Guy, probably because her Dad took time to show her wonders of the great outdoors. Mom and the Old Guy both told me stories about Grand-dad Cob when I was growing up. I barely remember Grand-dad Cob.
He was blinded in a construction accident when I was a very young boy. All I remember is being called to his bedside so he could feel the contours of my face shortly before he died.

The Old Guy told me Grand-dad Cob used to be quite a duck hunter in younger days. No wonder I caught this disease from both sides of the family.

Cob had a hand crafted wooden boat with hand made wooden oars and a half-dozen decoys he had carved out of basswood. His gun was a side-by-side double with Damascus barrels through which he shot hand-loaded brass shells using black powder.

Cob's gun, handmade fishing rig and an old photograph of Fire Chief Robbe and his men posing by an antiquated pumper truck are all that I have to remember him by.

It required supreme effort to row his boat from the shelter of backwaters around Bagley, Wisconsin to running sloughs where ducks used to fly not far from the main channel. Shots were never wasted. Most were probably "ground swatting" at birds which had pitched in on his decoys. Cob had a growing family to feed, and would accomplish this by any means necessary.

My Mother used to roll her eyes when the Old Guy would tell the tale of Cob and the catfish. Apparently Cob saw a large flathead catfish fanning back in the tules where he waited for ducks one chilly November morning. With any luck the family would eat well that night.

Cob snuck out of his wooden boat in leaky hip boots and herded the big flattie to a point where he could wrestle it into submission. The stunned catfish was thrown in the bottom of Cob's boat, he picked up the decoys and started the long row back to shore.

He was almost back to where his Model "A" Ford was parked when the catfish suddenly came back to life, flipping and flopping towards the low gunnels of Cob's boat.

Fearing food for the family might find its way back into the River, Cob decided to end the commotion by shooting the catfish in the head.

Magnum waterfowl loads were unheard of back then. But discharging a 12-gauge at point blank range will do some damage even with a low velocity black powder load.

Enough stomp came out of Cob's gun to kill the catfish and put a considerable crease in the bottom of his boat. He had to row like a man possessed to reach the safety of shore before the boat went under.

The saga of Cob and the milk cow is another story my Dad retold countless times. Cob purchased a young jersey cow to provide milk and other dairy products for Grandmother Alta and the kids. The cow should have produced ample milk for the family, but grandmother would seldom return back from the barn with more than a quart.

One morning Cob went down to the barn early and found out why. This cow was sucking on her own udder and drinking her own milk. Cob figured a yoke would prevent this from happening and went to work with his hand tools creating this restraint. He was so pleased with his work that he even made a three-legged milk stool for grand-mother to sit on while she milked the cow.

All appeared to be well with the world until Cob went to the barn the following morning to find the yoke was a mere inconvenience in self-milking.

Enraged, Grand-dad punched the cow in the ribs with all his might. This maneuver broke his hand and made him even madder. A swift kick to the cow's hindquarter broke Grand-dad's foot. He picked up the new milk stool and threw it through the window then hobbled and cursed his way back to the house.

Since Grand-dad was the fire chief the family had the luxury of an old crank-style telephone. Grand-dad rang up Slim Handel, the local livestock hauler and bellowed "Slim, get this teat-sucking s.o.b. out of my sight!"

Cob never talked that way around his good friend and fishin' buddy Rev. Seitner. They used to fish together almost every Saturday all summer long. The good reverend used to try his sermons out on Cob, knowing the only time he was likely to see the crusty old carpen-ter in church was at events like church suppers where my grandfather reined supreme as carver-in-chief of the main dish at the event.

I've always tried to offer my services to men of the cloth at no charge as a sort of ministry. Spiritual warfare is hard on pastors. They need time and a place to let off steam. There is no better place for this than the River.

I used to get a couple of pastors from the Madison area about once a year, but haven't seen them since they fought The Pike. We were having a decent day on the water. They talked shop a little bit in between catching bass and a walleye or two throwing crankbaits.

As we approached a deadfall near a point on the Minnesota side of the River, Pastor Walt hooked into a whopping big northern pike. The fish was all of 40 inches and every ounce of 20 pounds.

I eased the boat out away from shore and grabbed for the landing net, but Pastor Bill beat me to it, insisting on netting his friend's huge fish so they could better share the experience.

Pastor Walt agreed, although most of his focus was on the big toother which had his medium spinning rod almost bent double.

Suddenly, the fish tried to swim under the boat. Pastor Bill made a stab with the landing net. All he caught was one of the lure's two treble hooks which was not in the big pike's mouth.

This was enough of an edge for the trophy to gain its freedom resulting from outbursts from both gentlemen which had me wondering if they had left their demons on the dock or brought them along for the ride.

The book of Romans tells us we shouldn't do anything to make a brother stumble. Not much is said about providing the opportunity for stumbling. If Jesus could be out there in the desert for 40 days without any food and the Father of Lies persistently tempting Him, a man of the cloth should have no difficulty appreciating a beautiful autumn day chasing hungry bass with his wife.

My schedule was pretty tight, but it was clear Pastor Paul needed some recreational escape. I agreed to take Paul and his wife Barb out for a half-day on pool 9 the following morning.

Pastor Paul showed up with an impressive assortment of quality fishing gear. Barb had a pink custom made rod from a St. Croix rod blank and a Shimano Calcutta reel which was a birthday present just given by her thoughtful husband.

Paul clearly had ample ability to endure a little handicapping, subtly administered by his humble guide. Bass on a river often wait quite close to cover. In colder water they might not want to chase down a lure more than a foot away, even when they're in an aggressive feeding mood.

It didn't take much effort to position the boat where Barb had optimum advantage. She also listened to my suggestions when it came to lure selection, while her capable husband followed his own intuition.

Barb did an admirable job of putting on a fishing clinic for Pastor Paul, cooing over how nice her new fishing rod was as she lead yet another bass to the boat. After a couple of hours she had him down perhaps 15 fish to two, playfully calling this fact to her husband's attention. It was a message no man needs to hear from his wife.

The smackdown continued as we moved into the second hour on the water. It sounded like Paul muttered an epithet under his breath when Barb squealed the latest fish on the end of her line had to be every bit of four pounds.

We eased up on the downstream edge of a navigational daymark resting on rocks near the channel edge. Pastor Paul figured he was in the prime position to snake a couple of fish off of the rocks before Barb could make another cast.

Just downstream from this rockpile was a backeddy next to shore where water was just a little warmer and bass could hold with little effort. This was an easy cast for Barb, who connected on back to back 19 inch smallmouths.

Pastor Paul smacked his Rat-L-Trap on the surface, ostensibly to remove weeds from the lure as I netted Barb's second quality smallmouth. It was late October. Weeds aren't a factor on the Mississippi when leaves begin to fall like they are in September.

I distinctly heard Pastor Paul mutter a short adjective beginning with "s" and couldn't help smirking at the torment he must have been feeling.

We finished up drifting over weeds at the north end of DeSoto Bay. With a level playing field Pastor Paul started making up for lost time, hooking up on about every fourth cast.

Barb was pretty much worn out from combat with over 40 fish, including several huge and scrappy white bass. She took time to enjoy watching her husband find catharis from the fish, most of which were only 12-14 inches long.

Barb was only making one cast to her husband's five by this point. I didn't mention that a slower retrieve seemed to be more effective. Paul probably wouldn't have heard me anyway. He was intent on beating the water to froth in an attempt at self-perceived redemption.

Bigger bass liked the slower retrieve. Barb caught several more in the three pound class, chuckling quietly to herself with every fish.

Back at the boat ramp Pastor Paul gave me $150 for the trip, saying fifty bucks were for my expenses and the hundred was for a much needed lesson in both fishing and life.

I met Pastor Jim Ogden on a sandbar a few years ago when Dan Wabasha and I had Dan's two boys out waterskiing. Pastor Jim came sauntering up as Dan's younger son was putting on the skis and asked if I knew what time it was.

"Ten two," I replied, not missing a beat. "Ten two what?" Pastor Jim asked innocently. "Tend to your own business!" I snarled back. Pastor Jim looked like he had been slapped in the face by a very large carp, but recovered when he saw me grinning.

We struck up a conversation. I discovered Jim was pastor at a small Evangelical church. My wife Candy and I were thinking about moving back to the River about that time. Finding a church was an important requirement which needed to be met before we pulled up stakes.

Pastor Jim said he had never caught a fish on an artificial lure before he jumped in the boat with me. It didn't take long before the young pastor had multiple species to his credit, some of substantial dimensions.

He sent photos of his piscatory conquests out to his Dad, Randy, in Arizona. Randy came out to visit a couple of summers ago. A fishing trip with Capn. Ted was on his agenda.

To that point in our relationship Pastor Jim had yet to land his first walleye. I took them to a spot which had been holding some quality fish. It was a rocky closing dam at the upstream edge of an island just off the main channel.

There were a couple of large rocks about seven feet away from a red navigational marker which often gave up fish. I told Randy and Jim to cast their crankbaits about this distance away from the big

62

red buoy.

Jim's cast bounced off the channel marker. Randy's toss was right on target. A fat four pound walleye inhaled the lure and Jim's face displayed the slightest hint of a scowl.

When Randy found out that Pastor Jim had never caught a walleye, he proceeded to offer up a chop-busting only a loving father can administer to a son. Pastor Jim behaved like the man of God which he is, but his struggle to rein in comments and thoughts a loving son might express to his badgering father were palpable and nothing short of hilarious.

Pastor Jim said he used to do a little ice fishing with his grandfather when he was young, but that these times were primarily a chance for the elder Ogden to slip away and drink a couple of beers.

Jim got to meet my runnin' buddy Cal during his first bona fide Mississippi River ice fishing trip a couple of years ago. Cal has a heart of gold, but a sometimes joyfully evil sense of humor.

I was a quarter mile away poking holes in search of perch when Pastor Jim caught the biggest perch of his life, a very respectable 14 incher. He put this fish in his five gallon bucket eager to show off his prize when I returned.

Cal waited until Pastor Jim wasn't looking and swapped the 14 incher for a 10 inch perch. When I came stumbling back down the ice, Jim fished around in the bucket and pulled out his prize, looking quite perplexed.

"I thought my perch was bigger than this," he said dejectedly. Cal reached in his bucket and withdrew the purloined perch. "Look at this baby, boys! Now this is a nice perch!"

Jim knew that he'd been robbed but was at a loss for words,

falling back on a repertoire of facial expressions which quickly brought Cal to his knees in a fits of laughter.

Rank, privilege or social positions mean absolutely nothing when men are out there on the ice.

Dan Wabasha

Dan Wabasha

Dan Wabasha is like a wild-eyed 230 pound Labrador with muddy feet who is darn glad to see you. His sense of humor and lust for adventure knows no bounds, although he now ponders potential for disaster five or 10 seconds before diving in head first like he did 30 years ago when we first started running together.

Nobody works—or plays—harder than Wabasha. His folks had some money and left a fair amount of resources to Dan and his brother Dick when they passed on. Dan has never worn wealth on his sleeve. Most of the time his sleeves are rolled up and he is belly deep in some project which will either make more money or cause him to laugh from the soul.

Dan is a man of vision. He doesn't worry about possible consequences if his sharp eyes spot a $20 bill blowing across the grass on the other side of I-90 and the Hungry Gator moat is teeming with ravished reptiles in the median strip. He will find a way to get the money.

Dan surrounds himself with capable, practical people. I envy his natural ability to make friends. Should I happen to be the pal du jour when he shows me the money; my part of the mission is finding a way to negotiate the hazards so we can share in the eventual reward.

Most of our adventures are a quest on some kind of tangent to hunting and fishing. We discovered this common bond when not working on the Beloit Fire Department. We didn't work together much, because command officers assumed any personnel who had that much fun couldn't possibly be focused on saving lives and property.

This perception hounded us throughout our entire careers. But there were times when we would trade time or find ourselves on the same shift through some ripple in the grand design. Firefighters tend to be schemers with plenty of time to hatch a plan with several layers of subterfuge to conceal the true intent.

If Wabasha and I discovered we would be sharing the same niche in the mandated space/time continuum we would often game the system to end up on the same crew.

I made acting lieutenant before Dan did and forfeited my paramedic license shortly thereafter. Sixteen years of riding the Meat Wagon on an all too regular basis had me yearning to be a hose jockey again.

EMS runs are about 90 percent of the work load of most fire departments. This isn't bad duty during the day if some Asiatic captain makes the determination his crews not on emergency runs should be painting or polishing or suffering through some other mindless task.

If you weren't assigned to the ambulance there was a fair chance of sleeping through the night, or at least sneak enough shut-eye to make outdoors pursuits the following day more enjoyable.

Wabasha still had his paramedic license when I took a 24 hour hire back on his shift. Command officers invariably put the guy making overtime on the Meat Wagon if they could find a way to do it.

This time I was assigned to Station 2, a house with both an engine and an ambulance. Most days Station 2 was a three man billet, with the crew jumping the appropriate rig when an alarm came in.

Dan was a decent medic. But he didn't really like the work, hanging in there only because of a slight pay differential.

On this particular tour my assignment was firefighter, working the nozzle on fire calls and a glorified EMT go-fer if we had to leave the nest in that orange-and-white box.

Dan's regular job was engineer at the time. On ambulance calls he would serve as one of two medics. The "third wheel" was the lieutenant, an overweight, politically motivated guy named Byron Norbert.

Byron and I came on the job together about a year before Dan got hired. Byron and I went to paramedic school together, rode the ambulance a lot together and ate more than a little smoke in a hot and threatening environment when it was time to work this part of the job.

Early in our career I gave Byron the nickname "Wally" after WGN radio personality Wally Phillips. Byron loved to talk on the radio. He loved to be in charge.

Eventually he became a deputy chief. This promotion happened shortly after marrying the fire chief's daughter.

He earned the promotion pretty much on his own merit, driven by a hunger for that white shirt with gold bugles on the lapels. Wally developed a reputation for micromanaging the troops under his command. Boys at the firehouse say this tendency grew more severe after Dan and I retired.

Wally tried to throw his weight around when he had just one silver bugle. This never worked with Dan and me, probably because we had so many years of shared experiences.

On this particular shift Ambulance 12 got a call for a GI bleed. We arrived on scene and were greeted by a skinny older man who told us the patient—his wife—was upstairs.

Our noses confirmed this was indeed a GI bleed situation the instant the skinny old guy opened the door. Rabbits have the second stinkiest guts in the mammalian order.

Human guts smell much worse. A GI bleed smells like a human who has eaten rabbit guts and then developed a bowel obstruction for several days prior to calling the ambulance.

When the skinny old guy opened the door and told us the patient was upstairs we sensed an imminent encounter with Hannity's epiphany. Hannity used to run with Murphy and O'Brien.

Hannity's epiphany says: if a skinny guy tells you the patient is his wife upstairs, you can bet the farm that she will weigh at least 275 pounds. Of course this proved to be the case.

Wally, Dan and I were getting pretty close to the worst case scenario range for ambulance runs when we made patient contact and surmised this woman had been soaking in her misery for at least a few hours.

She had become dehydrated, in a cascade of symptoms which

quickly tumbled into a cardiac emergency. Cardiac emergencies are often preceded with loss of bowel and bladder control and spontaneous vomiting.

It was all Dan could do to keep from tossing his cookies from the olfactory overload of an overweight woman in a confined space with a GI bleed. When she threw up, Dan's response was immediate and spontaneous. Wally just happened to be in the way.

Wally had called for an engine assist shortly after sizing up the situation. When Engine 4 showed up, Dan wasted no time announcing he would help this crew carry the cot upstairs.

Wally and I had been down this street countless times before. Although our patient care was outstanding and thoroughly professional, it was all I could do to keep from laughing at the puke-splattered lieutenant and Dan's scalded dog exit from the emergency scene.

It took a good two hours to get back in service after this call. The patient survived.

We got back to Station 2 with a pizza picked up at my expense as the benefactor of overtime pay.

Wally insisted on critiquing this run. We laughed until we cried. There was a strong possibility of going off duty with a sore belly any time Dan and I worked together. We were like two monkeys in a barrel with a large flask of brandy.

A few years later in our career Dan worked back on my shift in a time trade so we could go fishing together the following day. Once again, our billet was Station 2. Our regular engine was down for maintenance, so we had the TeleSqurt, a master stream device mounted on a 1964 Pirsch chassis.

This rig was front line when Dan and I came on the job. It was an open cab, without even a seat for the firefighter. The firefighter had to stand up in a little alcove and hang on to the TeleSqurt boom for support when responding to a call.

I was lieutenant at Station 2 back then, Dan was working as the engineer. Our firefighter was young Andy Mueller, a rookie. Andy had heard stories about some of the notorious escapades Dan and I used to find ourselves in, and was enjoying the two-man comedy show when an alarm came in for a house fire on the west side of town.

Station 2 was on the near east side, about a half-mile back from a big hill with a busy intersection at the bottom where Henry Avenue crossed Highway 51 next to Rock River.

We jumped on the rig and headed for battle at a most rickytick pace. Dan was a fast driver and a good one. My boot pushed hard against the button on the floor, the federal siren screaming help was on the way.

A rookie is scared enough responding to a working fire call. Andy was squirrelier than most new guys. Dan stepped on the brakes as we roared downhill toward the intersection. The pedal went right to the floor.

"NO BRAKES!" He screamed above the wailing siren, looking over in my direction. Andy Mueller saw his lifeline quickly fading away. "NO BRAKES!" I chimed in. Dan and I looked at each other and screamed.

Dan did a masterful job of double-clutching and downshifting. We made a left turn heading south on Highway 51 essentially on two wheels, rolling to a safe stop along the curb.

I radioed dispatch, advising of our situation. We were out of service. I looked back at Andy. His hand had a death grip on the

TeleSqurt boom, his whole body was shaking and his color was ghastly white.

Engine 3 reported the situation as a stove fire, telling all other units they could clear. I told Andy we were standing down. He said he would need to change his pants before we went back in service. He wasn't kidding. The story was re-told at my retirement party. Once again, we laughed until we cried.

Most adventures happened away from the firehouse. Certainly enough material to turn this chapter into an entire book. Remember, Dan is the kind of person who tends to focus in on details, totally oblivious to anything else happening within his action circle. For decades I've chided him about being halfway to an Idiot Savant status.

Both components to this diagnosis are definitely present in Dan Wabasha. His observations regarding behavior of game and fish are nothing short of remarkable.

Wabasha owns a farm next to a county park in southern Wisconsin. He has invested time and resources driven by his remarkable gift of dreams and vision to create an idyllic outdoors playground for hunting and fishing.

I still call Dan "Grabbit the Rabbit" because he always wants more. In one case Wabasha worked his magic to obtain signed permission for hunting the county park.

Hundreds of geese used to rest in a large pond on the other side of the park, often flying over Dan's farm. One time a large flock flew right over his metal pole barn where we were working on some kind of project. Dan grabbed his gun, stepped out the door and slapped a big honker with a full pattern of "T" shot.

The goose fell like a 12 pound rock, landing on the pole barn's roof where it remained after creating a considerable divot.

Sometimes the geese would land on the infield of a ball diamond at the county park to feast on the sweet green grass. Wabasha observed this behavior intently and hatched a plan to bag some birds the following morning.

We grabbed a bag of goose decoys and entered the park. Dan set several on the pitcher's mound with a string of perhaps eight more between the mound and first base. We could hear geese getting anxious over on the pond.

Dan told me to grab my gun and jump in the first base dugout as he crawled into a dumpster perhaps 20 yards away.

Geese were starting to lift off the pond. "Don't shoot the scouts!" he hissed, voice echoing in the dumpster. I wondered if he was talking about the vanguard of feeding geese or Troop 52 on a nature hike.

Moments later three big honkers glided in and landed between the pitcher's mound and second base. The geese were wary, perhaps because none of the decoys were being cordial. I suspect the primary source of webfoot angst was the noise coming from the dumpster as Wabasha prepared to shoot.

Although I have never heard a truck-struck badger bouncing around on the inside of a kettle drum, I suspect it would sound something like the unholy percussion emanating from inside the dumpster.

Just as the trio of Canadas reached the conclusion they might be in jeopardy, 20 more birds cleared the treeline already locked up in final approach. Dan folded his two bird limit with consecutive shots, using his third magnum load to finish off my second goose which was trying to make it back over the trees to safety.

Wabasha is the best shot on upland game I have ever seen. Waterfowl require an entirely different application of hand-eye coordination to calculate an effective lead.

Although geese are bigger than ducks, hunters tend to shoot behind them because their flight is deceptively fast.

Gerald "The Bald Eagle" Cain revealed the secret to success to me 40 years earlier down in southern Illinois at the B & C Hunt Club in Union County : Lead the birds until it feels right, double your lead...then add a foot...and you'll kill 'em every time."

I passed this wisdom on to Wabasha one damp and foggy December morning in 1992.

The ground wasn't frozen yet around Durand in north-central Illinois. Several inches of snow had fallen overnight. The ground was warmer than the air causing fog to develop.

Dan whined that he had never shot a goose, practically begging me to take him to a spot where I had permission to wreak havoc on several thousand birds. The geese were working freshly picked corn just on the other side of a brushy fencerow.

Getting to a point where we could shoot required negotiating a half mile of muddy plowed ground covered with heavy, wet snow. Wabasha liked to call our hunting adventures "a romp in the swamp on workmen's comp" that year because I was recovering from several herniated discs in my back from an injury that occurred while fighting a house fire the previous August.

We finally arrived at a suitable ambush point. It didn't take long for a small flock of geese to come ghosting overhead. Dan shot behind them. Moments later another pair approached, I whispered the Bald Eagle's recipe for success.

Wabasha folded one of the birds up like an Arab's tent, then looked at me with his patented wild eyed goofy grin and laughed out loud.

The limit on Canada geese that year in Illinois was three. I didn't plan on shooting any, thinking about stumbling back to the truck across that muddy plowed field. I reminded Dan of this impending hike after retrieving his second 10 pound goose.

It was one of those rare days when feeding trumped the sound of a fog-muffled 12 gauge. Wabasha whispered he could hear more geese on the way, jamming two more magnum rounds into his Benelli scattergun.

Dan had filled out his limit, looking at me with sad puppy eyes in an attempt to mask his "Grabbit the Rabbit" attitude. I told Dan he could shoot my limit, but that he wasn't going to get any help carrying six big geese a half mile through a snow covered muddy cornfield.

It was another classic case of that $20 bill bouncing across the grass on the other side of I-90 with a moat full of hungry gators in the median. It took well over an hour to get back to the truck. I carried Wabasha's gun as a matter of gun safety rather than giving into his pleas that six fat geese were too heavy to carry.

Dan stumbled and fell at least a half-dozen times, swearing off goose hunting at least twice on our return hike. Back at the truck I actually burst into tears at the visage of the big sweat-soaked, feather-flecked 230 pound human chisel plow.

Wabasha's penchant for pulling other souls into his obtuse quests with rod and gun frequently backfires when folks from his outer circle of friends are involved. Such was the case once in northern Wisconsin when Dan painted a picture of ice fishing joy to a man he

74

hadn't seen since high school and a buddy of this childhood buddy.

Wabasha invited this duo to join us up on Pelican Lake at his Brother Dick's tiny cabin for a four day tip-up and jigging adventure. Neither of these two had a clue about ice fishing or inclination for sharing chores at fish camp.

We catered to them for two full days. Dan felt bad because I was essentially guiding with no chance for compensation. Rather than explaining ground rules to these guys and risking hard feelings, Wabasha opted to drown his sorrows picking up a 12-pak of beer and big bottle of Schnapps on the way out to the lake.

I heard an animated conversation coming from Dan's one man tent which was an amalgam of cursing and maniacal laughter punctuated by the sound of hops being liberated from aluminum cans.

A cold front had pushed through, essentially shutting down fish activity. I drove Dan's new Suburban back to the cabin as he initiated the leather seats with a half bag of Cheetos which somehow missed his jowl flanked mouth.

Back at the cabin Dan resumed his job as the self appointed cook, announcing the evening meal would be venison chops which had been marinating in a gallon Ziploc bag for several days.

Wabasha was functioning in an alcohol induced fugue state when he twisted the burner knob on the circa 1932 gas stove. He was about to turn the third of the stove's four knobs looking for flame when he recalled a match was required for ignition.

The ensuing epiphany created a considerable commotion when heat met fuel source. Dan was amused by the small explosion, undaunted in feeding his hooch inspired hunger.

After searing the venison chops on both sides Wabasha

slapped the meat unto a plate and lurched toward the small table which was focal point for many activities in the tiny cabin.

One of these activities was changing leaders for tip-ups from big treble hooks for pike to small treble hooks for walleyes. Several of these smaller hooks on eight pound test monofilament leaders were strewn across the table when we sat down to eat.

It took considerable effort to process this essentially raw meat. Five minutes into chewing the second bite I glanced over at Dan who was well into annihilating his portion like a glassy-eyed TroyBilt chipper/shredder.

Something wasn't right. A closer look at Wabasha's jowly face revealed a light strand of monofilament descending from his chomping mouth. At the end of this line was a little #8 treble hook inching steadily upward with Dan-O's every chew.

I jumped up and grabbed Dan's fleshy cheeks with both hands, making eye contact while blurting "Stop chewing!"

He returned from the state of catatonia enough to comply. I grabbed the fishing line which was almost to his chin and pulled a good foot of it from his mouth before the end of the line with a fair sized chunk of meat popped out, Dan gagging in the process.
Shortly thereafter he announced intentions to take a little nap.

This was not the only adventure with a #8 treble hook as the focal point. One summer afternoon I was in the pole barn getting my Lund ready for another guide trip when the phone rang. It was Wabasha.

"I'm hooked!" he barked, trying not to sound too panicked. It took several minutes to determine he had been on hands and knees cleaning out his own boat when a knee went skidding into a wayward

#8 treble.

The #8 is a very small hook. Even with maximum penetration it will only reach a half-inch under the skin. As noted earlier, Dan has the capacity to put life in micro focus. His knee was the center of his universe. The #8 treble had Dan's complete attention.

I told Dan to grab some needle nosed pliers, just rip the damn thing out and to call back if he had any further problems. Ten minutes later the phone rang again. Dan lived about 20 minutes away. I told him I would be there in half an hour.

Wabasha would have to pay for this unwarranted interruption to my overall program.

He was sitting at the kitchen table in skivvies, white as the proverbial ghost when I arrived. Joy, his ever-patient wife was at his side and concerned about the severity of what Dan assured her was probably a fatal wound.

What a wonderful opportunity to stir a buddy's angst and apprehension to a fever pitch!

I told Joy and Dan that the situation was even worse than they had feared; explaining that skin atop the knee cap was an extremely sensitive spot. Although Wabasha had been a paramedic for many years and certainly knew this was an outrageous fallacy, his knee was the wound site. The only worse case scenario would have been a huge 6/0 treble with all three barbs impaled in his pericardium.

I explained that removing this hook would cause incredible pain and possible loss of consciousness, with the tremendous potential for substantial blood loss. I told Joy to grab a bath towel to combat this possibility. She returned with two.

Dan squeezed Joy's hand when I tightened down the needle

nosed vise grips on the bend of the hook, announcing I would pull with all my might on the count of three.

Wabasha's jaw was clenched as he nodded approval like a rodeo cowboy about to leave the chute on a bull no man could ride.

"One!" I snapped, popping out the hook in the process. It took Dan five seconds to realize this crisis had passed without pain or loss of blood. He jumped to his feet with that classic goofy grin and tried to kiss me.

"I'm going with girls this week, buddy," I said backing away. Joy slapped Dan in the back of the head.

Both Cal Alden and I felt like slapping Wabasha another time when light footing off the ice on DeSoto Bay one balmy March day a few years ago.

Late ice typically offers the hottest fishing action of the entire year. The Mississippi ice which covered this 10 foot deep backwater was getting truly spooky as we worked back towards the shore with buckets full of fish to cross a plank connecting the quickly eroding ice to shore.

Cal is a cautious and extremely competent outdoorsman, although he does have a tendency to fall out of small boats, kayaks and canoes on a fairly regular basis.

Dan first tried to walk beside Cal, giddy over our angling success. Cal growled for Dan to back off, emphasizing the genuine danger of falling through the ice.

He then slid back by me, seeking confirmation that Cal was just being grumpy. I echoed Cal's sentiments, adding several firehouse adjectives Dan could understand coupled with the term "idiot".

Wabasha skulked ahead and got in line. We looked like the Beatles on the Abbey Road album cover, only we were wearing coveralls and carrying buckets.

Cal is lithe, tall and wiry. He approached our plank to safety like a jungle cat, quickly scampering ashore.

Dan eased up on the plank with a couple of tentative steps, allowing it to take his full weight without any apparent problem. He then looked at me with a "you don't know!" smirk and started bouncing on the plank.

The ice gave way on the second bounce, plunging Dan into icy chest deep water.

His eyes stood out on stalks with an expression of genuine fear and unwelcome enlightenment.

I fell right to my knees in a five minute fit of uncontrollable laughter.

Cal & Randy

Buddies

Even in these days of electronic wonder there are one or two kids in every small town high school who are consumed with passion for the outdoors. When I was a kid growing up in northwest Illinois, most boys at least dabbled in hunting and fishing. My interests were light years beyond that.

Dan Wabasha, Mike Blart, Cal Alden and Randy Deerfield grew up in other small towns and heard the wild wind whispering in their ears as well.

I've known all of these good buddies for at least 25 years. Wabasha and I became instant chums on the Beloit Fire Dept. Dan introduced me to Cal back in the mid-1980's. Cal and I have shared caretaking chores for this lovable character ever since.

Deerfield and I were travelling similar parallel trails in southern Wisconsin back in the day. Randy did some guiding and worked as a sales rep for Berkley, when their primary product was Trilene fishing line. This company is now called Pure Fishing and is a major player in the sportfishing industry.

I did some guiding and wrote outdoors stuff for a couple of weekly newspapers and the Freeport Journal-Standard. The old Fins and Feathers magazine bought the first magazine article I had ever penned shortly before Deerfield and I met on the ice of Lake Waubesa. I think the year was 1980.

The article was entitled Sculling for Ducks on Old Man River. It dealt with the Old Guy and one of his cronies, Beezey Guenzler—two kindred outdoors spirits from the generation which had gone before.

Beezey's old scull boat still had a mount for a "punt" gun—essentially small cannon used back when market hunting provided part of a river rat's income. The boat had come from Tony Miles who was almost 80 years old when I met him as a youngster.

We were duck hunting down in Stransky's bottoms in late December. The Old Guy had a bucket full of charcoal burning in the bottom of our pit blind for warmth. Tony must have thought the fire had gone out because he caught a chill and reached for a can of kerosene used to start the charcoal which the Old Guy kept in the bottom of the pit.

When Tony tipped the can, a streak of flame came up the stream of kerosene. Miles pitched it out of the pit. This unintended Molotov cocktail immediately caught the cornfield on fire, ending our hunt for the day.

Although this event occurred over 55 years ago, I can still visualize the look of horror on the old duck hunter's face as he tossed that can of flaming kerosene. December duck hunts are always exciting. Some hunts are more exciting than others.

Fishing Hall of Famer Spence Petros introduced me to Blart. Spence used to be an editor for Fishing Facts magazine. After interviewing me about crappie fishing on the Mississippi for a Fishing Facts article Spence and I hooked up. He introduced me to Blart, who was in his fourth or fifth year as a pro football player.

Football caused Blart to put his love for hunting on hold for the 12 years he was in the NFL. Most of our early adventures were spent on the water or the ice. Since he retired in 1995, Blart has made up for lost time with gun and bow.

Most of my buddies probably wouldn't mind if I used their real names in this book. The exceptions are Wabasha, who has some concerns that his reputation as a profoundly successful businessman might be damaged if the world found out he is just a big kid who has to struggle constantly to maintain a façade of maturity and responsibility…and Blart who should have his brain studied in great detail when he finally goes down the big chute.

Blart is an extremely intelligent, very thoughtful giant of a man. He is a true gentleman to casual acquaintances, but is often a raging, babbling freakazoid at times around his small but devoted cadre of friends.

The limelight experience of being a pro athlete has never appealed to this quiet woodsman. He learned early on—and with good reason—that the press is not to be trusted. He also learned that everybody wants to be your friend, most angling an agenda with some kind of personal gain in mind at your expense.

Those few who have passed Blart's bizarre vetting process have the fellowship of a truly good man with a soft and compassionate heart, well protected by a brusque and truly tough exterior.

One of the gifts God gave me frequently manifests as one of my biggest flaws—a deep insight into personal peccadilloes and hot button issues coupled with a sometimes sharp and vitriolic tongue. The spirit is willing but lacks modulation.

There have been a couple of instances where Alden and Wabasha were so mad that they didn't speak to me for months. Deerfield is a tremendous diplomat, adept at hiding his goat and seldom letting on that you've captured it until this allegorical creature has gnawed the seat covers off of your truck.

Blart has been groomed since childhood to be anger motivated. A passive demeanor is not conducive to longevity in a career as a professional football player.

Why would anybody standing just 5 ft. 9 in. tall try to antagonize an angry giant into a fit of rage? Blart is fun to watch when he morphs into Incredible Hulk mode.

One time we were on a winter fishing trip down to Louisiana. Our guide, Daryl, was busy whipping up a roux with eight rabbits, figuring correctly that Blart would eat at least a half-dozen of the critters.

The giant was in a playful mood, calling me his "little Irish lucky charm."

Blart knew he was getting to me, and he loved every minute of it. For some dumb reason I decided he needed a little attitude adjustment.

Mr. Blart

"Say that one more time you big, bald Kraut and I'm gonna punch you right in the nose!" I growled.

Although his six-foot, five-inch, 275 pound heavily muscled frame was certainly quaking in fear, he hid it well. In a boast of undoubtedly false bravado, he thundered back "Oh, is that so, my little Irish lucky charm!"

The River Rat Code left me no alternative. I took a swing at his big pumpkin pie face landing a blow on his cheek with all the power of a buck field mouse accosting an African lion.

Next thing I knew he was spinning me over his head like a 10 ounce baton and slamming me to the floor where a meaty knee pressed my head while meaty knuckles jack hammered into my right thigh.

In a final gesture of education he grabbed my underwear which had crept up above the belt during his centrifuge move and ripped it off like he was pull starting a 25 horse Johnson outboard.

He then made the mistake of thinking I was whipped and let me stagger to my feet. "Oh, no...the Mad Jack look again!" he snorted. It was obvious Blart had had enough. I allowed him to slurp down his six cottontails in peace.

A year later we were planning the next Louisiana adventure. I advised Mike to start hitting the speed bag and lifting weights because Round Two was fast approaching.

"Yeah, I was just thinking about that the other day," he laughed through the phone "sort of reminded me of my high school days, wrestling with those fat little Wisconsin girls in the back seat of my car."

Round Two didn't happen that year. I won't bore you with the details of being stuck 10 miles from the boat ramp off the coast of Louisiana with no forward gear on Daryl's outboard and not another boat in sight.

He had just picked up his big Champion bass boat after having it detailed. The electronics, bilge pumps and other critical gear had been disconnected, with wires in a Gordian knot beneath the good captain's steering console. We didn't make it back to fish camp until well after dark.

There is much more to the story than that. Much, much more. The Louisiana trip is always an adventure. The year after that Daryl assured us the NO TRESPASSING signs we passed on dry land as we flew through the bayou in his Champion boat did not apply to us.

This made sense. In Wisconsin nobody owns the water. Wisconsin is not LaFourche Parish, Louisiana. Fifty square miles of this

Louisiana county are owned by the Plaisance family.

This family has so much money that they sued the state of Louisiana in federal court over ownership of the water and won.

Mike Plaisance informed us of this fact when he told Daryl to proceed to the Bobby Lynn Marina where he would be charged with trespassing. Plaisance had mercy on the two Yankees in Daryl's boat.

Bayou folks are like River Rats. We headed for the Bobby Lynn Marina simply to see what kind of cards Plaisance was holding. Daryl was issued a ticket by the Harbor Police, which Plaisance informed us that he owned.

The next morning Daryl talked with local folks from the town of Leeville. He decided not to fight the ticket when told the four judges in LaFourche Parish were named Plaisance, Plaisance, Plaisance and brother-in-law of Plaisance.

Blart and I were just thankful that we didn't spend the weekend cooling our heels in the Thibodaux jail after driving a thousand miles to find adventure.

Most of the time there is enough adventure close to home to hold our interest. If not Blart's provocative philosophy of life usually provides enough fodder for a memorable outing.

One time we were catching a nice mess of perch through the ice on Pool 9, finding plenty of action using small jigs with plastic tails. Blart believed we could catch even more perch if we had some minnows and insisted we stop at the bait shop to buy some before heading out on the ice.

I told him that plastics were enough for me and had him drop me off before continuing on to the bait shop. There wasn't much snow on the ice, so cleats were necessary to keep from taking a fall.

When approaching the holes which were so productive the day before I slipped on the slick ice but was able to regain my footing. Perch were still there and fairly active. I was able to slide two or three into my six gallon bucket before Blart returned from the bait shop and parked on Highway 35 about a half mile away.

The little devil which sometimes dances on my right shoulder told me to back off about 30 yards from the hot holes and conjure up a scenario to fell the angry giant.

Mike didn't have any ice cleats on those size 13 feet. It took him quite awhile to shuffle tentatively out to our hotspot carrying all of his gear and a small Styrofoam bucket full of minnows.

When the hot holes were about the same distance between us I yelled "Mike! Stop!" He complied immediately, knowing full well the sometimes dangerous nature of Mississippi River ice.

"You used to be an athlete, Mike. The hot holes are between us. How 'bout a race—first one to the holes gets to fish them?"

At the word 'Go' we both sprinted toward the hotspot. I sprinted for about three steps and stopped. When Blart got close to the holes it looked like he was trying to walk on ball bearings.

His feet splayed in different directions, the minnow bucket went up in the air and the angry giant performed a truly inspiring epileptic Macarena before his head hit the ice and minnows came down like rain.

Blart said some very unkind things as he stooped to pick minnows up off of the snot-slick ice. Every comment caused my gut wrenching laughter to cascade another notch.

He was absolutely correct about the minnows catching more fish. But if Ringling Brothers had a clown act like that they would still be on the road.

The following winter Cal Alden talked us into a quick trip out to Devil's Lake, North Dakota. Between Alden, Blart, Deerfield and myself we took quite a potpourri of venison sticks, jerky, dried venison and other treats to snack on

We spent more time fishing a couple of smaller sub-impoundments close to the big lake than on Devil's Lake proper, catching quite a few jumbo perch on jigging sticks and nice northern pike on tip-ups.

Alden used Deerfield's fillet knife to open up a heavily packaged quick-strike rig, gouging his hand in the process. Two days later Cal had a profound infection which required IV antibiotics. I had developed a substantial case of gout from essentially an all meat diet and Blart had blown out his knee chasing after a tip-up.

We decided to cut the trip short by a couple of days, since Deerfield was the only member of our fishing "A" team which was not wounded. I wrote a column about this adventure, with the slightest nuance that Blart was the one who suggested we retreat, thereby being the first to wimp out. This trip was five years ago. He's still mad about that slight.

All three of these guys are extremely well rounded, accomplished outdoorsmen. They got to this point in life by following their own intuition down their own personal trail.

Deerfield and Alden are both licensed guides in Wisconsin. Deerfield has done considerably more guiding than me. When my primary career was working as a firefighter, Randy was guiding fishermen on the lower Wisconsin River and the Madison chain of lakes.

He has built up a phenomenal client base over the past 30 years, with a great deal of return business. Randy seldom gets a day off from April through October. Like Wabasha, Randy is a "people person."

A major difference between these two friends is that Randy has a more analytical, pragmatic approach to success in the outdoors with the patience to teach skills and techniques so subtly that clients don't even realize how much they are being guided.

Dan wouldn't pay attention to lightning striking the ground all around him if he were watching a great big brown trout fanning in a pool and he just happened to have a corn dog in his pocket.

On some basilar level Dan probably realizes that lightning and storm clouds mean a tanking barometer, with a lifetime of experience whispering fish might want to hit aggressively.

He might reason that cornmeal is a tempting meal for some fishes like carp or channel catfish and that the wiener inside might resemble a bloated nightcrawler. Chances are the scarred up old brown trout had never seen a corn dog floating along in its home pool so why wouldn't it work?

Conventional wisdom, common sense and experience all scream that only an idiot would use a corn dog for a trophy brown trout. Dan focuses right through these inconveniences. If one brown trout in a gazillion was somehow moved to eat a corn dog with a hook in it, Dan Wabasha would be the guy who would find and catch that fish.

Randy would have no problem fooling just about every other trout in this mythical stream and enabling a client with little more than basic skills to at least tussle with a few of them.

If Blart found a hidden stream just teeming with trout he wouldn't tell anyone else. Instead, he would belly crawl to an optimum spot at night and make every attempt to fish without being detected.

Cal is extremely selective in his guiding work. Although he "guides, assists and directs" others he doesn't take any money for the work. Cal's Dad died when he was very young. He learned many of nature's ways through exploring on his own or with his two brothers Karl and Joey. He also had several outstanding mentors along the way and is on a mission to pass this legacy on to some in similar straights who have a fire in their belly and limited means to find their way.

Cal has an extremely altruistic personal code of ethics and beliefs which he tries to instill in those he might teach. He has little tolerance for folks who take an opposing view.

Several years ago he was on a passionate tirade about deer license allocation in a neighboring state. His argument was sound and I agreed with most of it. However, belaboring the point on this issue was futile because Cal lacked the pathways to bring folks in the neighboring state the wisdom of his epiphany.

The little devil on my right shoulder whispered this might be a fun topic to tweak him on just a little bit. Cal got so mad he jumped out of my truck and stormed back to Dan's deer camp a mile away in frigid temperatures wearing nothing but jeans and a flannel shirt. He didn't know I was playing. When Dan told him this was the case he refused to believe it. Cal didn't even speak to me for two months. The gift of discernment can be a cruel curse if you allow it to be.

Cal, Blart and I are all pretty much like lone wolves or haggard hawks. There are times when we come together to hunt or fish. Little needs to be said about tactics or techniques because we have all reached common philosophies of action and procedure from individual experiences.

The best illustration of the relationship Alden, Blart, Deerfield and I share is found in bowhunting. Bowhunting is a solitary sport. Putting yourself at a time and place to ambush a trophy whitetail buck and making a clean kill on a consistent basis requires woodsmanship and hunting savvy in the extreme.

Every fall we go into different woods together, later relating details of the hunt to each other. There is no jealousy when one of us bags a Booner buck. Rather, a vicarious thrill enjoyed by all.

It is almost like we were the ones who saw that long-nosed doe look back several times and grunted in just the right cadence to nudge the Big Boy into making a vulnerable appearance 19 yards from where we have waited patiently, scent-free and totally focused for three hours before the moment of truth arrived.

The Old Guy had a crew which included Beezey and Bower. Somewhere out there in the heartland are three or four kids in small town high schools who will eventually meet on the common ground of the great outdoors and become fast and forever friends.

My generation didn't have the freedom the Old Guy did. The next generation will have an even more restrictive maze to navigate, but they will surely find a way.

The Mississippi Queen approches Lansing, IA.

Plugged in

Some clients ask if they can bring a portable GPS along to mark hotspots. This request never fails to make me smile. The River is only about a mile wide, runs essentially north and south and has huge navigational daymarks with mile boards at regular intervals along the main channel.

Wiser clients bring a map, overjoyed when I mark areas where we found success and other potential honeyholes they might prospect at a later date. Maps are just a variation of the old fishing excuse "Ya shoulda been here last week!"

The Mississippi is forever changing. Some changes are extremely subtle. Others are nothing short of profound. It is a hermaphrodite of evolution: you can call the Miss Old Man River or refer to it with feminine inflection as in "She is sure in a generous mood today.

This force of nature is more than a living thing. It is herds of living things, each with an agenda perpetually morphed by every other living component in the sum of the whole.

Countless books have been written about the Mississippi. My personal favorite is George Byron Merrick's Old Times on the Upper Mississippi, first published in 1909. It is subtitled "Recollections of a Steamboat Pilot from 1854 to 1863."

My Mississippi certainly has a different face than Merrick's, with 33 massive lock and dam systems forever changing her face over the past 80 years. Her irrepressible soul remains unchanged. Man can impose his will for a short time. But the River will always persevere.

Cal Fremling's work Immortal River takes a more scientific look at the Upper Mississippi, chronicling the forever flow from ancient to modern times. William Burke's The Upper Mississippi Valley looks at how the landscape shapes the heritage we live with today.

Every one of these tomes whispers our fleeting encounter and insignificance with a life force literally older than the hills. Native Americans took in the grandeur from bluff tops at a place we now know as the Effigy Mounds just north of McGregor

Marquette and Joliet witnessed the undeniable hand of the Creator as the first white men to see her naked beauty less than 300 years before I first tasted the rich, musky air on a humid summer evening.

I still revel in breathing deep this hearty River aroma, filling my lungs with her spirit. She has possessed me since I first became aware of more than just immediate surroundings.

It wasn't until I was tumbling rapidly towards six decades on the planet before realizing the holiness of this place. The Mississippi is the finest example of God's majesty that I have so far experienced.

The honesty and intricacies of the River are far beyond my comprehension. I accept the River by faith, born from grace just like I accept the Holy Bible as words breathed by God.

God's truth swims in every minnow and every molecule of water in the perpetual and perennial panorama of forever.

In Mark Twain's historic Life on the Mississippi, the legendary author and bona fide River pilot notes that the Mississippi is growing forever shorter, pulled by the life force of gravity with the irrepressible power of water pushing away lands that stand in the way.

There is a new cut up in Minnesota slough which was born through this process in the summer of 2010. Even the most modern maps show the stretch downstream from Visager's landing as solid ground.

The reality of this cut flows almost nine feet deep with the River running at what is now referred to as normal summer pool. It was cut by current somewhere between flood stage and outrageous in the high water which showed up in early July and stayed until winter.

Walleyes, saugers, bass, panfish and flathead cats adjusted to the changes quickly. It took me just a little longer. Two weeks after that the word got out. Some fools probably have the place plugged in as a waypoint on their GPS.

This little niche is certainly different than it was back when it was land in June 2010. Pool 9 was so clear that June that local news media made it a lead story on more than one occasion.

I was in awe after walleyes completed spawning and eased

94

back downstream about the 20th of April. The marble-eyes always spawn about the 20th of April on this little snort of River. At least they have for the blink of time that I've been out there chasing them.

By May you could see down a good five feet on the main River channel. TV host Dave Carlson called, sniffing out another segment for his Northland Adventures show.

I get a kick out of working with Dave. He's so serious about his craft. Cameraman Dave Roll and I love tweaking him, acting like a couple of jovial deer flies all day long.

This crew showed up in June, filming in the first imbedded rain we had seen in weeks. Even with overcast skies Carlson could see a big rock where I said a big smallmouth bass had been cruising earlier that day.

He deftly wafted a Tee-Kee-Lee fly to the shadow of this rock and was rewarded with 20 inches of acrobatic bronzeback bass. Roll caught the entire encounter on videotape. Sometimes it all comes together.

The skies opened up before the segment aired. The River got tall and dirty and stayed harsh and surly until the tundra swans moved out.

These huge white waterfowl show up between Brownsville and LaCrescent about a week before whitetail deer go into full blown rut. They come down from the arctic and feed on roots of plants we call duck potatoes to fuel for the next stage of their annual fall migration.

The swans don't continue down the River like so many other winged creatures. For reasons known only to God, they take a hard left here and vector toward wintering grounds around Chesapeake Bay.

Two days after they go, backwaters start locking up for winter in a substantial freeze. Just like walleyes spawning around April 20th, the tundra swan migration is one of those little winks nature gives folks who let ambition go in an attempt to plug into the grand design.

"Tundra Swans getting ready to migrate."

I have spent countless hours in tremendous turmoil searching for patterns in fish behavior which might be exploited for the edification of clients and fluffing of my substantial ego.

Leaving all the demons at the dock and easing out in an attempt to plug into the grand scheme of things is always more productive than being hampered by plans and calculations driven by the last time out on the water, for each day brings a new River.

The Mississippi is not one river. It is many rivers, with a half-dozen tributaries becoming part of the flow as the River eases downstream through every designated pool.

By the time she passes LaCrosse these tributaries, streams and rivulets might be imagined as individual wires of different colors and sizes in a massive living wiring harness of a jumbo jet with size beyond comprehension.

Factor in the influence of the sun which will change the flavor of the River on the east side or the west side depending on time of day. Factor in the influence of the moon, the barometer, the wind… environmental variables are countless and ever changing.

Fish respond to this enveloping input by simply swimming, responding to perpetual changes in a visceral attempt at survival. Those who believe they can master the vagaries of fish behavior and motivation are only fooling themselves.

There is much to be said for just goin' fishin'. The journey might begin as a species specific pursuit for walleyes, catfish or bass. With considerable effort you might just find success with walleyes or catfish or bass.

But by plugging into what the River is trying to tell you the rewards will reveal themselves without conscious effort and you will find yourself thinking it's all good.

My Lund Alaskan has a GPS as part of the electronics package. The feature is seldom turned on. Any person who guides on water running essentially north to south that is less than a mile wide should know exactly where they're at with only one eye open.

The only exception might be in late summer when cooling air temperatures over a still warm River often create fog of incredible density. The fog is usually gone by 9 a.m., taking an active fish feeding window with it, so there is much to be said for being able to navigate in this extremely low visibility environment.

Following previous tracks provides a degree of comfort in telling you where you've been. The real hazards are drifting logs and similar flotsam -- and towboat traffic out on the main channel which holds the very real potential for tragedy.

My eyes are almost always on the River rather than the GPS during heavy fog conditions, with comfort found in familiar stumps, points and similar landmarks while underway.

My Humminbird gear also has a surface temperature feature. This is handy in the spring and fall when slight changes in temperature can make a world of difference in fish location.

Most of the time neither of my sonar units is ever turned on. One of the most important aspects of being plugged into the big picture is the ability to read the water. Riffles, foam trails and other features all have meaning, just like they did when George Merrick was in the 'Texas' of a steamboat before electronics or even harnessed electricity.

With the exception of walleyes and catfish, most fish folks want to catch are usually active in less than 10 feet of water, with cats and marble eyes spending most of their time lurking within a couple feet of the bottom.

In either instance being able to look at the water with a fair hunch on what lies beneath the surface is just as important now as it was a century ago. Time on the water is the greatest teacher in this regard, with low water levels generally found in late summer the best time to learn.

High water in June can hide a little knob of rock that's high and dry in August. Knowing the exact location of this structure when fish think it might be a real good place to spend some time certainly stacks the odds in your favor.

A basketball sized rock can create a place where many fish can hold with little effort on the downstream side. It's seldom a good idea to leave active fish to go find fish on the other side of things, if fish aren't holding where you found them yesterday or an hour ago it doesn't mean they won't be both present and eager a little later in the day.

Every single fishing trip is different. It's a brand new ball game every time. Don't make the mistake of thinking fish will be where you found them almost suicidal just the day before.

The old Mississippi is always a new River, easing out there and listening when she whispers her mood rather than drawing on your own perceived expertise is the best way to start catchin' instead of just fishin'.

"Darrin found his first 10 pound walleye hiding near a wing dam."

Bam Bam & Pebbles

If this chapter title causes a flashback to the animated off-spring of Rubble and Flintstone, you are probably a child of the 60's. The adjective "flashback" certainly took on different meaning before that decade came to a thundering conclusion.

The first Earth Day was celebrated in 1970. I was attending college at SIU in southern Illinois back then, discovering new and exciting outdoors opportunities while my 16 foot flatbottom and purple-cowled Evinrude gathered dust in a Carroll County barn.

Since that time the altruistic environmental movement has been hijacked by folks bent on using Mother Earth's protection as subterfuge for much more ominous intent. Meanwhile, the Big River keeps on rollin' — but it certainly isn't the same River I knew as a kid.

Some of the best fish producing wing dams on the upper ends of this pool are pretty much silted in now. Work is done on wings and other structures every summer. This process has been ongoing since 1907 when Congress authorized the Army Corps of Engineers to maintain a six foot channel on the Mississippi River.

Every year I get two or three clients who want to learn about wing dams, either because they've felt the bam-bam of a new propeller smacking rocks and a sound like pebbles in the gear case of their lower unit and want to avoid another encounter …or they've heard that wing dams are fish magnets and seek keys for unlocking the piscatory treasures which cruise there.

Wing dams were the precursors of massive lock & dam systems placed in the 1930's to improve navigation and assist in maintaining what is now a mandated nine foot channel. Wing dams still help serve this purpose as deep thinkers still employ short sighted methods which result in long term, disastrous consequences downstream.

This situation is not unlike the new government mandated eco-friendly light bulbs, the ones which look like curly fries. The new bulbs are supposed to last much longer than Edison's bright idea and save energy in the process.

Look at the packaging of these bulbs and note where they were manufactured. Then look a little closer and read the government warning. The new eco-friendly light bulbs contain mercury.

Break one and you will be exposed to toxic mercury fumes. Disposal of a broken bulb is a small hazardous materials exercise, with the potential for fines and possible imprisonment at some time in the future for failure to properly dispose of a broken light bulb which

101

was mandated by the government!

This certainly wasn't the intent when we danced around in tie-dyed tee shirts to the sound of bongo drums and acoustic guitars on the first day of Spring, 1970. Shipping jobs to China so they could poison the slaves that we've become to their economy wasn't exactly what we had in mind.

But it is what it is. Those who truly love the earth in this country have dropped the ball. We are passing this mess on to the next generation. The least we can do is provide a twist out of Dickens's A Christmas Carol with ghosts of the Mississippi in the past, present and truly ominous future.

Back when the Flintstones cartoon occupied most of my higher thought processes you could launch a boat across from Palisades state park and easily get out to the main channel on pool 13 through any one of a half-dozen cuts out of the backwaters.

Now there is just one narrow, ponderous route which must be maintained by frequent dredging. The problem is siltation coming down from upstream. Siltation has all but killed the diversity of pool 13 where I grew up in the span of just one generation.

The situation downstream is even direr. Long stretches of the middle Mississippi are essentially dead from a fishing standpoint. Kids growing up in central Illinois, Iowa and Missouri simply accept the situation as it is without a scintilla of outrage over what the River used to be.

The Palisades is a little north of mid-pool on pool 13. This 30,000 acre stretch of River runs from the dam at Bellevue, Iowa to the dam at Fulton, Illinois. There are still a couple of worthwhile wing dams at the northern end of the pool, but the fishery is a mere shadow of what it was just 30 years ago.

Savanna is a popular site for bass tournaments today. Largemouth bass tend to grow larger than smallmouth bass. Largemouth bass can thrive in silted in backwaters.

Smallmouth bass require better habitat.

The first five pound smallmouth bass I ever caught slurped in a minnow near a driftpile of logs back in Lainsville slough back in the early 1960's. This fish got put on the stringer an ended up on the table. Catch and release was unheard of back then.

If somebody catches a three pound smallmouth on pool 13 in these early years of the 21st century it will be from waters within two miles of the Bellevue dam. It will take photographic evidence to prove such a catch. The fish will likely be released, because this is what we do now.

Will this fish survive and grow to five pound trophy status? You might take a minute to ponder the possibility. I've spent years contemplating this situation and it hurts every time I get close to facing the truth.

Meanwhile, life is good upstream on pool 9 where I spend most days drinking in the grandeur of the River either with my trusty Lab Hanna Banana or with clients.

At first glance the Upper Mississippi is in great shape. Muddy Mississippi? Not here. At least when the River is stable between flood and other high water events. When the River sleeps during winter ice you can see 10 feet down into the water column.

Five foot visibility is not uncommon between rain events in late summer. There are now places where desirable weeds like coontail take root along the main channel edges in more than 10 feet of water, providing habitat for countless species of life.

This is a good thing, right? Not necessarily. The water column is clearer now than it's ever been—at least to a certain extent—from an invasive species called the zebra mussel.

Like other mussels, the thumbnail-sized zebra is a filter feeder. It has few natural predators besides a duck called the scaup. This dark colored diving duck, a.k.a. "bluebill" used to come down the River every fall in much greater numbers than we now see in the early 21st century.

"Are Bluebills the next threatened species?"

When they push back north in the spring the migration corridor is much wider, perhaps 50 miles on either side of the River rather than the 10 mile wide flight path seen in the more purposeful fall migration.

Springtime means a lot of flotsam will come floating down

104

the River. In recent years there has been a noticeably larger funeral procession of dead ducks. Almost all of these dead ducks are scaup.

Biologists are telling us mortality in scaup is coming from a small parasite. Should we be concerned? If you were working in a coal mine and saw a canary suddenly go belly up would you hang around down there until air quality improved?

Zebra mussels were doing just fine even before the scaup started dying off. They found suitable places to live on top of native mussel species which have been in the River for as long as there has been the River.

When I was a kid there used to be over 20 native mussel species. Now there are just five or six. It is what it is. But what will it be?

Folks sharing my boat can count on getting an earful of information about these dilemmas and numerous other subjects when we're anchored up above a wing dam looking for fish.

Wing dams are essentially rocky fingers which extend out at about a 90 degree angle towards the channel from shore or close to shore.

Anchoring up is a productive method for catching a number of different fish species on pool 9 and points north. Every wing dam has a personality which changes through the seasons and with ever-fluctuating River levels.

Fish are drawn to wing dams because food can be found there. The strongest motivation for fish behavior is the predator/prey relationship. This concept is a can of worms in its own right which we won't delve into just yet. Worms are part of the predator/prey relationship. So are crawfish, insects, amphibians, minnows and larger fish.

All these creatures sometimes wind up near wing dams as

a by product of man's attempt to maintain a nine-foot channel for navigation.

Some clients seek specific information on fishing wing dams. Answering specifically would be like using one profile to describe 10 guys named Larry.

There are, however, some rules of thumb which might help you decipher the mysteries of a wing dam.

One key is a general guideline of holding your boat along the eight foot contour when fishing above a wing dam. This requires one eye on the electronics while another eye watches riffles which are sometimes visible downstream from the top of the wing dam while you keep another eye on the client's behavior and another eye on the client's rod tips.

Guides with only two eyes often find it easier to anchor up with the stern of the boat at the eight foot contour, where most clients can easily reach the top of a wing dam with a moderate cast.

Exact position is driven by current flow over and around sweet spots which every productive wing dam possesses. Wing dams are not placed with laser precision. Often a pile of rocks gets dumped a short distance away from the major portion of the wing dam, or there is a spot just a little bit lower at some point along the wing dam which might act as a forage-feeding chute when the River is at a certain level or any one of a half-dozen other scenarios which will drive fish location and activity levels.

Although wing dams are generally placed at a 90 degree angle from the channel, the current doesn't usually flow directly downstream over a wing dam as it does on a smaller river dumping over a low head dam.

Some current will bounce into the face of the wing dam and then flow towards the channel end of the structure with increased velocity, working toward the intended purpose of maintaining the nine foot channel.

This variable needs to be considered when anchoring up, which is a procedure that might take several attempts before the boat is in an acceptable orientation to permit bait or lure placement with a reasonable chance for success.

Livebaiting is often a productive presentation when anchoring up above a wing dam. There is much more to this aspect of fishing a wing dam than throwing a fat worm out below a sinker and kicking back until a hungry fish swims along.

A "river rig" is a popular offering when anchored up above a wing dam. The bait can be a half-crawler, fat leech or minnow. Bait selection is driven in part by water temperature and time of year.

The centerpiece of a river rig is a three-way swivel. This small piece of metal has little eyelets to tie lines to at the end of three short shafts extending out from a central hub.

One line is tied to the main line which runs back to your rod and reel, one line is 14-26 inches long with a hook and bait with the remaining eyelet tied with a 4-8 inch dropper line with some kind of weight to hold the offering close to the bottom where a fish is liable to swim by if the boat is anchored up in an acceptable position.

Exact lengths of the two dropper lines are driven by water clarity, current flow, bait selection and a couple of other variables. The dropper with a hook can be just a hook, a hook with an orange bead in front of it, a hook with a spinner blade or a hook imbedded in a soft floating jighead—or several variations thereof. The dropper with weight is usually some kind of banana-shaped sinker. Banana shaped sinkers are less prone to getting hung up on the rocky face of a wing dam than sinkers of other designs.

If the productive livebaiting presentation du jour is casting and making a slow retrieve rather than "deadsticking" and only moving the bait a foot or so every now and then a jighead with either another morsel of livebait or a plastic tail or a bucktail can be a better option than a banana sinker for weight. The logic here is simple: many fish get caught on jigs, few get caught on sinkers.

Sometimes casting crankbaits is more effective than livebaiting when anchored up above a wing dam. If you're fishing a crankbait correctly, the lure will occasionally chunk into the rocks.

Getting hung up is inevitable. One way to minimize hanging up is to remove the front treble hook from the crankbait. But if you're fishing where the fish are, you'll eventually find the rocks with the crankbait.

Crankbaits are expensive, $4-6 a copy. Throwing five-dollar bills away looking for a walleye dinner is a pretty expensive path toward a full belly. About 70 percent of the time allowing considerable line out to create a belly between the rod tip and the lure will result in freeing your tackle from the obstruction. Ten percent of the time this maneuver results in hooking up with a fish, provided you're fishing where the fish are in the first place.

The other alternative is pulling in the anchor and sliding downstream in an attempt to free your crankbait from the rocks. There is a real strong possibility that this will result in revisiting the bam-bam/ pebbles mode with either the outboard motor or less expensive but more fragile plastic blade of a trolling motor propeller.

Once you get the lure back — or break the line in the process — all you have to do is motor back upstream and try to reposition the boat in a productive orientation driven by current and location of the wing dam's sweet spot.

This book is not about fishing tactics. The previous digression about just one method and presentation for fishing a wing dam is intended for those readers who are not avid anglers.

If this passage were written solely for avid anglers there would need to be considerably more detail required to inform and educate this old guide's method of putting a worm in front of a walleye under specific conditions.

Clients drive the conversation on any given outing. Discourse can range from master's degree intensity on livebait presentation to "take this rod and try to cast the bait over there" to a rant on those curly-fry lightbulbs and the downfall of America or favorite cartoons of the 1960's.

Every day on the Mississippi is a brand new adventure.

"Quiet riffles sometimes hide obnoxious rocks."

Beyond the channel

Every year I get one or two new clients that are well rounded outdoorsmen who "just want to learn the River". This desire amounts to a first date with a very pretty girl which might mature into a lifelong relationship.

In the 40 years my precious wife, Candy, and I have been married we have gone through considerable changes together. She was just 18 and I was 20 when we tied the knot.

The Old Guy had to go with me went I went to the County Clerk's office to obtain a marriage license because I was not yet of legal age.

As we stood waiting our turn at the counter the Old Guy asked me if I knew how much a marriage license cost. I'm sure he saw me reading a sign which said "Marriage licenses $10, Death certificates $2.

Math has never been my strong suite, but this problem had an obvious answer.

"A marriage license is ten bucks, Dad," I beamed.

"Ten bucks and every cent you make for the rest of your life," he growled back with a couple of well-placed adjectives in this statement of fact which made other customers in the County Clerk's office look at him and stare.

The Old Guy was just trying to look out for me. Contrary to my wife's insistence that profanity is just a lazy man's way of being emphatic there are times in the language of men when interjection of colorful words ensures quicker response or reaction in matters of great importance or perceived danger.

When I was on the Beloit Fire Department from 1979-2001 there were many instances where response to dangerous situations or imminent equipment needs made use of colorful language acceptable.

When flames are licking at your boots through an ice covered and slippery roof and your crew is tasked with vertical ventilation saying "Excuse me, Larry...would you please hand me that pick-point axe?" just doesn't seem to cut it.

Experiences on the Mississippi frequently elicit man talk from clients. I try to maintain a civil tongue, but there have been times under extraordinary circumstances requiring a timely response that I've slipped up.

Sometimes an epithet is the ideal response but you find yourself in a situation where words fail you. A smallmouth bass trip with an elderly gentleman several years ago comes to mind.

Jack had average angling ability but an incredible passion for chasing smallmouth bass. He preferred ultralight tackle. His favorite wand was a seven foot GLoomis IMX rod with a buggy whip tip.

This outfit enabled him to cast small lures great distances. Several bass had already fallen victim to a #1 black Panther Martin spinner when Jack observed a small ripple on the surface 75 feet away which he thought might be a feeding smallmouth bass.

He wound up to make a snappy backhand cast and stuck me right in the cartilage between my nostrils. The little Panther Martin spinner immediately received my complete attention.

Rather than turning to see what obstacle prevented the extremely sharp hooks of his little lure from continuing on toward their intended destination, Jack simply pulled several times on his whippy spinning rod.

My surprise and pain was far too great for either tears or profanity. Later I had insight into how Pinocchio must have felt after telling a whopper. But shortly after the moment of impact my entire concentration was on grabbing Jack's four pound test line before he made another serious tug.

When my client finally turned around to better assess the situation his face went immediately pale as he gazed at my face in slack-jawed horror.

A little blood was dripping on my shirt from the injured schnozolla, but the pain had subsided considerably after tension on the lure had been removed by breaking the line.

Jack insisted we go right to the emergency room. I wasn't

keen on him drive my rig 40 miles to LaCrosse and having my boat sit in the parking lot with hundreds of dollars worth of gear vulnerable to theft.

I told Jack to take my needle-nosed pliers and remove his lure from my nose which was not needlesque, but most certainly longer than when I got in the boat that morning.

He said he couldn't do it. Bleeding had stopped by this time, replaced by persistent pounding which told me my pulse was roughly 72. We had just over an hour left on the trip and I insisted that Jack get back to fishing. He caught a couple more small bass, looking back at me and wincing about every third cast.

The spinner dangling on my upper lip held most of my attention until we got back to the boat ramp and Jack paid me with profound apologies and a hundred dollar tip. I got to keep the spinner, too.

It just took a second to remove the bait from my face with needle nosed pliers and the truck mirror to direct the procedure. This seemed like an appropriate time for profanity which was somewhat muffled by the bloody fishing towel beneath my nose.

My apologies for digressing from the analogy that an initial Mississippi River experience is like a first date with a very pretty girl. Some recollections of life out there can be painful and recurrent.

Those who enjoy a long term relationship with another person will tell you both individuals experience considerable change with the passage of time. The Mississippi has certainly changed since we started dating, but her changes are slow and subtle. The human component of this relationship learns something new with every single encounter.

Most of the fishing experience on the Mississippi is found beyond the channel markers. In late winter and very early spring the channel edges are a good place to vertical jig a minnow-baited buck-tail for saugers and the occasional walleye. From late September into late October drifting a bluegill along over the same bottom can result in brutal combat with a big flathead catfish.

Flatties often hold in deeper holes off the ends of certain wing dams along the downstream edge. Sturgeon can provide a good pull in the fall when they slurp in a couple of nightcrawlers from the bottom on the leading edge of a scour hole below one of the dams. But for the most part, fishing begins where the channel ends.

Back before the massive lock-and-dam system was put in place at Genoa in the late 1930's the Mississippi had several major side channels as it coursed downstream towards Lansing, Iowa.

There is a relic channel on the east side of the River between a closing dam a mile or so above the Highway 82 bridge which extends a half-mile downstream into Winneshiek slough.

Across the River and upstream is another old channel in a serpentine backwater known as Minnesota slough. The deeper holes aren't as deep as they were 20 years ago. But there are still places where the bottom drops away into more than 30 feet of water.

The River must have been a sight to behold in Grand-dad's day before placement of those 33 locks and dams changed things pro-foundly and forever.

I have a Coast Guard issued captain's license which allows me to take up to six persons in a boat up to 99 tons out on the Missis-sippi River. Back before the Coast Guard started regulating things in the early 20th century requirements for a captain or pilot's certifica-tion were much more stringent.

There were no aids to navigation like channel markers or daymarks back then. Early steamboats didn't have effective searchlights to pick out hazards in their path. The boats often ran at night, with pilots navigating by closely observing the shapes of bluffs along the River coupled with readings from a weight and sounding line on the bow of the boat.

Moonlit nights required different navigation skills than those when the sky was dark. Pilots had to possess the ability to look at the water and know with certainty which riffles meant deep water and which meant hazards from a shallow shoal.

Sandbars, shoals and snags are still hazards to navigation just as they were back in the heyday of steamboats from 1840-1870, but modern day captains have those aids to navigation and sophisticated electronics to guide their travels out there on the main channel today.

There are no aids to navigation once you cruise beyond the channel markers. Even the most sophisticated sonar gear is of little value when running with a fair degree of speed back in the sloughs. The ability to read the River is just as important now as it was when legendary steamboat pilots like Captain Thomas Burns and Captain Daniel Smith Harris worked this water in the early 1800's.

Entry into the Upper Mississippi's myriad backwaters and sloughs is frequently obstructed by a rocky structure called a closing dam. Like wing dams, the main purpose of a closing dam is diverting the lion's share of current to maintain the nine-foot-deep channel for navigational purposes.

Closing dams may run across the entire mouth of a slough or just along the upstream entry point. Some closing dams are below slough entry points to control erosion, with several "dragon's teeth" which are essentially small wing dams inside the mouth of sloughs with considerable flow.

The upstream edges of islands off of the main channel are also frequently protected by rocky barriers. Every one of these rocky structures holds the potential for outstanding fishing opportunities, with success driven to a great extent by River levels and seasonal concerns.

Many of these closing dams are visible or even partially out of the water when the Mississippi is flowing at low pool levels. July and August usually provide the optimum opportunities to learn the idiosyncrasies of these rocks which can become fish magnets when hidden by the Mississippi when she is in a more robust mood.

One of these closing dams and a run of rip-rapped shoreline directly across the River on pool 9 gave up 14 smallmouth bass over 20 inches long back in the summer of 2009.

These fish fell to a variety of presentations primarily driven by time of day. Shade is often a positive factor in the summer months. Tall bluffs along both sides of the River provide shady hiding places on the Wisconsin side of the Mississippi until almost noon, with Iowa/Minnesota shorelines typically better from 2 p.m. until nearly dusk.

You might think this pattern would change with overcast conditions, but it doesn't. At least not very much if River levels are stable.

Some entry points into backwaters and running sloughs are nearly blocked with shallow sandbars which drop away quickly into deeper water. These areas can be ambush points for a variety of gamefish species early and late in the day as both baitfish and predators feel emboldened by lower levels of light penetration.

Terns, gulls and other birds often provide a key to both fish location and activity levels. If you see a bunch of gulls sunning on a sandbar they are probably waiting for shad or other food to appear. No point in fishing nearby just yet.

If the birds are dipping and diving towards the River's surface waste no time in getting over there. Feeding frenzies are most common during low light periods, but they can occur at any time.

Savvy River Rats keep a rod with a topwater bait or an in-line spinner like the Mepps Black Fury handy to cash in on one of these often spontaneous feeding opportunities.

Backwater islands and pseudo-channels are forever changing beyond the channel markers. The most detailed map will only tell you what was there on the day the map went to the printer.

Being on the water almost every day is the best way to stay current with the River's ever-changing currents, but this is big water. It may be weeks before you revisit some of the necks and nether reaches.

I rarely get lost on my home water. But there are occasional moments of bewilderment when water which was four feet deep becomes a mere four inches. A keen eye will usually decipher humbling shoals and flats before wading becomes a part of the adventure.

Serpentine sloughs like the Winneshiek are like a trammel net. The farther in you go the shallower waters become until you discover there is no easy way out. Sloughs often offer a series of options as you enter from the upstream side.

Every backwater point holds a choice between forks. Both options will take you downstream. One carries more water and is easier to travel. Spending a couple minutes studying options is always a good strategy if you haven't been there in awhile.

If a point has a driftpile, snag or community of crawdad caves it is always worth a cast or two, even if you can see the bottom and the water is only inches deep.

Backwater channels where water is at least four feet deep right next to weeds like sandgrass and arrowhead is a great place to probe for bass and pike. Runs of backchannel with at least eight feet of water can produce amazing summer catches of walleyes.

Conventional wisdom might tell you walleyes would be most prevalent and active somewhere along the main channel or cruising the upstream edge of a wing dam when serious summer arrives in all its pungent, heavy glory.

There are always walleyes out there on the main River. But you'll often find more willing fish back there in the sloughs.

The diversity of life beyond the channel is nothing short of amazing. Dragonflies, butterflies—and deer flies. Beaver, muskrats and otter. Ducks, Redwing blackbirds, hawks and eagles. The Upper Mississippi is home to lots of eagles.

Clients are thrilled when shown an active eagle's nest with a couple of fuzzy heads sticking up from the tangle of branches in a tall and sturdy tree.

I almost wrecked the boat once taking in the River's grandeur with Hanna Banana who has benefit of that keen Labrador retriever nose. Two eagles were sparring high overhead in a preamble of their midair mating ritual.

Suddenly the white headed birds locked talons and began tumbling toward the earth, pulling out mere feet above the water just yards ahead of the boat. Just a few yards beyond their dramatic exit from the dance a huge stump loomed. My brief visit to Dan Wabasha's world could have had a nasty outcome.

The summer of 2010 began with the River flowing profoundly

clear. Rains and high water arrived about Independence Day and stuck around until the tundra swans pushed south and the River eased along under a blanket of ice again.

High water allowed unprecedented access to areas which would be little more that wetlands during a "normal" summer.

I was seeking some channel catfish for a guide trip later that week, carefully winding through the back channels of Minnesota slough. A right turn and a left turn brought me to a new side channel about 50 feet across with just enough water to hold active channel catfish, but not too deep or swift.

In the middle of this channel was the heavy trunk of a long dead tree with a young bald eagle perched on the root system, a bewildered look on his face. I anchored up about 25 yards above this snag and tossed out a couple of lines with dipbait to see if any cats were home.

The mother eagle arrived a few minutes later with a fish in her talons and started chiding both me and her offspring. Twenty minutes later the mature bird determined I was no threat and glided down gracefully to land on the fallen tree not 25 yards away, leaving a 13 inch walleye on the main trunk of the tree before flying back up to her initial roost to keep an eye on things.

The brown-headed juvenile eagle hopped down from the root system and swaggered parrot-like up to the little walleye. I could hear the bones crunching as this raptor ate his lunch. Of course I had no camera in the boat.

Back home that evening I told my wife about this encounter, making plans to return the following day on a fish seeking and reconnaissance run. The young eagle was still there!

It was that time of year when eagles goad their young into leaving the nest. Junior must have floundered and was fortunate enough to land on the dead tree instead of in the water.

A young eagle learning to fly

I anchored up a little closer this time. Maybe 10 yards away. The mother eagle began her scolding again, with considerably more voice—probably the eagle version of colorful adjectives.

I was about to pull the anchor and sneak off to a vantage point which was a little less invasive when the huge white-headed predator swooped down to a stump at the edge of the water.

Remaining quiet and motionless is usually the best option when entering the woods as a predator or observer. The mother bird cajoled her youngest in a tirade of yellow-eyed angst. If there was such a thing as eagle profanity, this was definitely it.

The mature bird took wing and screeched inches above the

juvenile's head with talons down, landing on another stump on the opposite bank.

Her baby took the hint, clumsily attempting a vertical takeoff. Wingtips brushed the water as untested wings pumped in a struggle for survival. With little more than a yard to spare the eaglet crashed into saw grass a few feet from her mother's perch.

I quietly lifted anchor and eased away. Two days later I was sharing this story with the client as we motored slowly toward the fallen tree which marked a young eagle's first attempt at flight.

Just before we made the final turn in the slough, I saw this bird sitting next to its parent 50 feet up on the bare limb of a silver maple tree. Travel beyond the channel often reveals the Mississippi's greatest treasures.

Not all sheep are wooly.

You can't beat a drum!

The last thing a guide wants to hear is "A bad day fishing is better than a good day at work".

This usually means fish aren't biting as aggressively as they imagined on a Tuesday afternoon when they would normally find themselves behind a desk, a steering wheel, in the barn or on the shop floor.

Those who have never hired a guide often imagine guiding to be the best job in the world—essentially not even work at all. Fishing is supposed to be recreation, care free, flat out fun...having a great big cake and eating every bite without shame or remorse.

It is my job to ensure they leave my boat still believing fishing is all lollipops and rainbows. I do everything in my power to make client's time on the water a positive experience.

Truth be known, my power doesn't extend much beyond tying on a hook and telling folks where to cast. The finned critters which we pursue are not tied up. They have basic motivations for going where they go and doing what they do at certain times, but Jesus is the only guide I know who can get into the head of a fish 24/7 and see that you get hooked up every time.

Time on the water is the most important factor in consistently catching fish. Even if you're on the water every day, the best indication of their behavior is only as good as the last cast which produced a little action. Other fish have moved on since then, either physically or in feeding attitude.

Sometimes the cast which produces a fish will lead you to hone presentation just a little bit resulting in another fish which strikes with even more vigor. Sometimes not.

All a guide can do is coach the client on his best hunch regarding where the next willing fish might be and what might tempt her into dancing.

This can be extremely hard work, especially if the client is less than proficient with a rod and reel or even realizing what a bite feels like. Even if a client is an avid angler with good gear and all fishing factors are in positive alignment the only thing this person has total control of is his or her attitude.

If somebody says "do you guarantee fish?" our first stop will be at a bait shop for some minnows. You want fish? Minnows are fish. Cross that clueless question off your list.

I know it's going to be an interesting day when somebody who professes fishing knowledge makes an initial cast with a spinning rig then reels backwards with the spinning reel on top of the rod.

There have been times when I'm working my outdoor writer gig in the boat of another guide I've never met and purposely made a clumsy cast followed by this misuse of fishing tackle just to get a reaction out of the guide.

Most folks who hang on every word from an outdoor communicator think that every one of them is an expert who can 'walk his talk'.

Truth is, there are three kinds of outdoor writers: Some write but can't fish, Some fish but can't write...and a few who can do both and do both well.

Guides who deal with outdoor writers are well aware of this fact, doing everything within their power to validate the writer's impression that he is a legend in his own mind.

The first thing a guide does is size up his client's ability. If I see a look of disgust and concern on a guide's face after a couple of clumsy casts I like to follow up with something like "How heavy of a string do you use on your winders?"

If this question is answered with presumption of canine ancestry on my mother's side I know we're in for a good day on the water.

As I tumble willy-nilly into my 60th year on the planet, I am working through my 38th year as a licensed fishing guide. I've been regularly writing outdoors stuff for almost that long.

These dual pursuits lend themselves to VIP treatment from sporting goods companies in the form of free stuff or product at greatly reduced prices. The outdoor writer break is typically better than any deal a guide might cut as a professional angler. But I make it clear when agreeing to be listed on a manufacturer's "Pro Staff" that the emphasis is placed on my abilities as an outdoors professional rather than as a communicator.

The writing gig takes me all over the map. I've fished all over North America, most of the continental 48 states, oceans on either side, the Gulf of Mexico and four of the five Great Lakes.

I live — and guide — on the Mississippi River because it is the most challenging, humbling and sometimes productive water which has ever seen my hook.

Clients often ask "what is your favorite fish?" With over 100 species swimming in the Mississippi you might think deep and profound consideration might be called for before answering that question. Nope.

My answer is quick and jubilant: Sheephead! Some folks call this homely piscator a sheepshead. Some call it a drum. Down in the Louisiana bayou you'll often hear this fish referred to as a gaspargou. In the Midwest sheepies have a number of different appellations, many of which should not be heard by ladies and young children.

I love 'em because they are always willing to bite, offer a real good pull and are just as good as any perch or walleye next to beans and fried potatoes. What more could any angler possibly ask for?

Tie into a sheepie on the heavy side of 10 pounds and you will call him both Daddy and Mr. Sheep before the battle ends.

Put a smaller one in the boat and toss it right on ice and you have the key ingredient for a spectacular fish dinner. The key to rave reviews in preparing any fish or game dish begins with how you handle the meat.

Keeping sheephead cold is the first step. Filleting away red meat on the skin side of the fillet and the red 'mud' vein which runs along the drum's lateral line is the second. Clean, hot oil is the third, cooking fillets no more than 90 seconds on each side. Make sure the oil is popping hot by flicking a drop of cold water in the pan before getting down to frying.

My favorite fish breading is as easy as catching these wonderful fish. Simply put equal parts pancake mix and cornmeal into a gallon Ziploc bag with a liberal dose of salt, pepper and garlic salt. Shake 'em up, fry 'em and serve with a poker face telling the little white lie that fresh caught walleye is the best eating fish around.

There are days when the River is at flood stage, a northwest wind is howling at 30 mph, a massive hatch of mayflies has peppered the water or the Old Man is simply in an ornery mood when the lowly sheephead has saved both my bacon and the day.

For this reason alone I will always defend the sheephead's honor, whispering enlightenment to folks who would offer a disparaging remark when the feisty bass, walleye or catfish at the end of their line morphs into a sheepie somewhere between the hookset and the landing net.

Drums are scavengers. You may find them chowing down on minnows beside a school of hungry walleyes, scarfing up crawdads out from a mud point in a backwater dotted with "snakeholes" where bass have foregathered or smashing a crankbait intended for pike.

My personal best sheepie was over 30 pounds. She hit a Timber Tiger crankbait intended for bass in a cut just off the main channel near the town of Victory a few years ago.

I was fishing with Jesse Simpkins, who was pre-fishing for a Team Supreme bass tourney scheduled for the following weekend. We were fishing out of Simpkin's heavy bass boat which this sheepie was able to pull around with the authority of a big MinnKota trolling motor.

Sheephead often occupy the same areas which feeding walleyes find appealing, intercepting the half nightcrawler or minnow fished on a ballhead jig intended for a marble-eye. Big walleyes will often shake their heads when hooked. Sheepies sometime do this too, but you can usually tell the difference between a sheephead and a walleye just a few minutes into the fight because sheephead fight harder.

Weather conditions and River levels are usually pretty stable between June and September. Bass are almost too easy to catch. So are catfish. Walleyes can be a little tougher, especially in the heat of summer.

My favorite clients are those who just want to go after whatever is biting. If they want to take a mess home for a fish fry we'll usually go after panfish. When they catch enough bluegills, crappies and perch to fulfill this goal there is often enough time left in the trip to find success on bass or pike, maybe walleyes.

I have two regular clients who love going after big flathead catfish in the fall who insist on chasing sheepies when booking a trip in the summertime. Habitat for fall flatties and summer sheepies is similar: main channels edges and deeper holes with a fair amount of current.

My favorite summer sheephead rig is a half-ounce purple or

chartreuse bucktail river jig tipped with a half-crawler and trailing a #8 stinger hook. Good sheephead water is never more than a mile away from virtually any point on the main channel of the Upper Mississippi.

On those days when I'm not guiding and have the need to feel a good pull I know a willing sheephead of substantial dimensions is less than a 15 minute drive from home and a five minute boat ride from the closest ramp.

If I'm fishing alone launching the boat and parking the truck won't take more than four minutes, ditto recovering the watercraft for the trip home. When I'm fishing with one of my buddies time spent at the boat ramp is almost always less than a minute, probably closer to 30 seconds.

One of my biggest pet peeves is people who lollygag at the boat ramp. Some simply lack experience with backing up a trailer. Some back their trailer into the water too far then have trouble centering the boat on the trailer to pull it out.

A good rule of thumb is backing the trailer until the trailer is in the water just past the axle hub and/or the first couple inches of trailer bunk or sternmost rollers are underwater.

If you are a casual boater and get nothing more out of this book, please read the previous paragraph again, then mark it with a yellow hi-liter and dog ear the page, refreshing yourself with this pearl of wisdom just before you back up and block the ramp!

There is a learning curve in boat ramp etiquette. I give folks benefit of the doubt, first offering assistance in launching their boat either physically or by friendly suggestion.

Looking back over the years I'm ashamed to recall at least two instances where I felt the compulsion to use knuckles as a boat ramp etiquette education tool. At the time of these incidents my only regret was probably the lack of a substantial Louisville Slugger ball bat.

There is only one way to get to heaven. This is through believing Jesus Christ died for your sins, was raised from the dead, and now sits at the right hand of God, the Father.

I must admit at one time some of my motivation for seeking salvation was to avoid an eternity of waiting at the boat ramp for some cheerful jack-wagon to either launch or retrieve his boat.

Although I strive to live a Christian life and the days grow ever shorter before my pulse departs and eyes open to reveal heaven as my beloved Mississippi there will certainly come a time when the opportunity arises to turn the other cheek at another's boat ramp faux pas.

If the nitwit in this scenario is not sincerely repentant and capable of resolving this situation in a timely manner there is still enough heathen in me to at least attempt a physical attitude adjustment. It doesn't matter how big and tough they are.

Are you listening Mike Blart?

Hanna's first Grouse.

Hanna Banana

Hanna Banana is my last dog. She is also the best dog I've ever had—or even seen. This evaluation may be somewhat subjective. My buddies say I have an unnatural affection for this gorgeous 74 pound yellow Lab. Hanna and I both know better. Those who would speculate otherwise are not members of our pack.

Hanna is the alpha female. I am the alpha male. My wife, Candy, is a lesser female with utility only when Hanna feels like taking a walk or as a bunkmate when Hanna begins her nightly conquest of Candy's king sized bed.

She starts this maneuver in a lower corner, quietly slipping up on the covers with a Chihuahua-sized footprint which will expand to a territory suitable for a magnum sized Great Dane before the clock strikes two.

Unlike most Labrador retrievers, Hanna has little compulsion for seeking approval or affection, at least from anybody but me. When we're indoors she is seldom more than 10 feet away, always attentive like a canine Secret Service agent tasked with protecting the president.

Communication between us is frequently on a telekinetic level. She senses I am thinking about her and moves closer to be of service. Sometimes she moves closer because I have not been receptive to her attempts at canine mind control or attuned to her desire for food, a walk outside or affection.

If close proximity fails to get my attention she will treat me to either a paw on the knee every minute- persistent like a smoke detector with a low battery- or the heavy head, with which she can exert at least 90 pounds of silent persuasion commanding an instant gaze into her caramel brown eyes.

Leaving her at home for guide work or some other task requires penance. She will hound me until I drop what I am doing and lay in the floor in a submissive position from which she can bark out her superiority, delivering a series of mini-bites like a normal dog pestered by a flea might do.

She knows I will always be the alpha male, submitting to her temporary dominance as merely a show of mutual respect and common affection before resuming my role as Canine Commander.

Hanna's veterinarian says she is quite comfortable with herself, displaying no apparent need for human interaction. Forget about dialog with other dogs. Hanna does not believe she is a dog, seeing herself as a four-legged, heavy tailed superior evolution of a human.

To her mind there is only one other living entity in this exclusive species: me.

We are usually far beyond any mention of verbal commands like sit, stay, heel or kennel.

She simply knows when it is time to perform these functions and follows through with little need for more direction.

Not that we don't talk. Experts will tell you that communication with dogs is supposed to come in the form of short, one word commands. Anything else is just a waste of words. Most dogs hear "Fido, blah blah blah, sit."

Hanna understands complete sentences, although there is wisdom in limiting the number of words in the sentence and number of syllables to three, at most four if we happen to be discussing an extremely complicated subject.

Her understanding of vocabulary is at least a couple hundred words in English. Probably an equal number in Mandarin Chinese. I'll never know because I don't speak Chinese.

If I'm in a hurry to go someplace and want her to hydrate before we leave I will say "Hanna, thirsty." She will drink, even if she doesn't feel like drinking because she knows the pack is about to go on some kind of exciting mission.

"Be a good dog" is the communication for relieving herself; she does this on command. "Poop" is a command which may take up to five minutes to obey. I'm envious. It sometimes takes me twice that long, even with copious and regular consumption of fiber.

She sits in the passenger seat of the truck. If Candy is along Hanna grudgingly moves to the middle of this bench seat. On a longer drive she will eventually place her paw and then her head on Candy's leg, making it perfectly clear that this is an imposition and that my wife should be honored to act as a pillow.

When we arrive at a destination Hanna will not leave the truck until I say "okay". She will not walk far beyond arm's reach unless told "hunt 'em up" or "check it out".

She might leave a considerable puddle of drool on the hardwood floor of our kitchen if a T-bone steak was placed there, but she wouldn't dream of even inching closer to the steak until permission is granted.

This kind of blind obedience never required corporal intervention, a shock collar or seldom more than a stern word. Ever since she reached enlightenment at about five months of age we have had a mutual understanding.

Hanna would have achieved Perfect Dog status at four months if it weren't for an incident on Kinkaid Lake in southern Illinois. I was doing a story on muskie fishing for Illinois Game & Fish magazine. Hanna was well along in her watercraft socialization training.

Guide Al Nutty was using his MinnKota trolling motor to ease us close to a point which held the potential for a big fish from the stern of the boat, controlling our path with a foot peddle connected by a long cable to the motor on the boat's bow. Credit puppy tendencies for investigating the chewability of that cable. Thankfully this was only a hundred dollar faux pas.

My mistake, but Candy insisted Hanna take the blame because we would still have the hundred bucks if I hadn't insisted on bringing Hanna along.

Experience teaches the wisdom of letting Hanna take the rap in my wife's eyes. If you want a long and happy marriage it is critical to have the last word in any disagreement. This word should be an exact response or acceptable variation to "yes, dear."

Hanna insisted we go with a cordless remote control in my Lund guide boat to avoid the clutter of cable on the deck. What a smart dog. She knows what is expected of her and almost always does it well.

There are similarities in raising dogs and kids. Both undertakings hold both joy and pain. Mistakes will be made, but mistakes should diminish as experience increases.

Candy and I have always had Labs. The first was a yellow dog named Jill. She wasn't a pure Lab, but the Labrador genetics were overwhelming. Back in 1973 Jill hunted up and fetched 73 ringnecks for me during the Illinois pheasant season. There were a lot of birds around back then. We hunted almost every day, and certainly bagged our share.

My buddies liked to call Jill "the government retriever" for her regrettable tendency of removing 20 percent of a gamebird's breast before delivering it to hand. I blame myself for her hardmouth tendencies.

If you want a soft-mouthed dog don't play "fetch the stick," then pull the stick away from the dog's mouth so the game can continue.

Jill had a couple of other flaws. We used to let her roam free at the house in the country we used to rent when I was working as a weekly newspaper editor. This practice ended when a neighbor called and said my dog had killed a couple of his sheep in cahoots with another neighborhood canine.

Like many clueless parents I at first refused to believe Jill was capable of bad dog behavior of this magnitude. Strands of wool in her teeth said otherwise. Travels were limited to the length of rope tethered to a stake near her dog house except when we were hunting or fishing after that.

Jill's partner in crime was dispatched with a well placed round from a .223 rifle the next time it came trotting down the lane.

Jill only lived a year or so after this incident. On one of our outings she must have gotten a scratch from a rusty barbed wire fence. The vet said she had lockjaw. After two weeks of suffering and low prognosis for recovery I gave her an intentional overdose of the sedative the vet had prescribed.

We buried Jill behind the barn after placing two long pheasant tailfeathers on her quiet yellow body and firing a three round salute in the air with the shotgun which was such a joyful part of her life's work. I cried like a baby, howling at her death from my very soul. That was nearly 40 years ago. There is more than one tear in my eye as these words are written.

Rufus was my next dog. Until Hanna came into the picture, Rufus was the one good dog every man is entitled to in his lifetime. She was not without her faults; most flagrant and fragrant was an all encompassing joy from encounters with skunks.

On one duck hunting trip to Saskatchewan she tangled with four polecats in a single week, the last soiree coming about an hour before four of us piled in a big Dodge van to drive a thousand miles back to the Midwest.

Rufus was born back in 1976, about the same time our oldest daughter Jessica came into the world. I made many more mistakes raising Jessica than were suffered through with Rufus. Rufus lived to the ripe old age of 14.

When it was clear just getting around caused considerable pain we made that long, slow drive to the vet. The last thing she did was put her blocky black head in my hand and wag her tail. Tears back then. Tears right now.

Rufus wasn't a very good mother, raising only four pups out of her first litter and just three out of the second. Spooky was one of those pups. His dad was Haverhill's Black Shadow from the renowned Haverhill kennels out east.

Shadow belonged to a buddy of mine. He got pick of the litter. I got Spooky. Three years into his life Spooky looked like he had what it took to be an even better hunting dog than either one of his parents.

It was August and we were getting ready for what had become an annual duck hunting adventure up in Saskatchewan. Spooky suddenly came up a little lame on his left front leg for no apparent reason.

The next morning I went out to his kennel and noticed one eye looked like it was developing a cataract. We immediately went to the vet. His diagnosis was blastomycosis, an almost always fatal disease which develops from spores in the soil, often found around wetlands near beaver feces

Despite aggressive treatment Spooky's condition worsened. He was a young warrior who never really had a chance to get in the fight. I opted to give him a warrior's death. Shooting your own dog is one of the toughest things a man can ever do.

Tubby was the next Lab to come into my life. She was a stray which showed up on our doorstep about two days after we just moved into a new home in the country.

Getting another hunting dog was a major focus of my agenda

when we finally got out beyond noise from horns and sirens. I believe Tubby was a gift from God. Like many dogs which get dropped off in rural areas due to some serious character flaws in their former masters, Tubby had abandonment issues. she was a very nervous dog, constantly seeking attention and reassurance.

Good dog!

Tubby wasn't much of a hunter, but she did manage to flush, find and retrieve a few birds. I'll take at least part of the blame for Tubby's lack of excellence. Working three jobs to support my growing family meant there wasn't much time for the two of us to become a cohesive unit.

Tubby lived to a ripe old age of undeterminable length. She lost considerable weight and developed difficulty getting around. I dug a grave at the back end of our property and we took that final, painful walk. Tubby got a warrior's farewell with my .22 pistol.

I vowed not to get another dog until retiring from the fire department, a goal which was realized on June, 2, 2001. Hanna was born on August 21st of that year.

Buddy Jim Webster and I were greeted by a litter of cuddly, rambunctious Lab puppies when we pulled my boat out of the water near Cassville, Wisconsin. about Sept. 15th of that year.

Few things on this earth are cuter than a tumbling mass of Labrador retriever pups. Four of the dozen little dogs were yellow females—just what I was looking for.

A couple weeks later I conned Candy into taking a drive over to the River. Enroute the ulterior motives for this road trip came to light. If any yellow female puppies were still available our now empty nest would have a new arrival.

We stopped for a chicken dinner along the way and left the restaurant with a smudge of chicken grease on my favorite cammo hunting hat. I was nervous as we drove down the gravel road over that final river bluff.

Three puppies were already spoken for. Two yellow females were still up for grabs, both the epitome of cute.

Kneeling amongst the pups I took off my hat and threw it a few feet away.

Hanna was the only puppy paying attention to this move. She immediately cavorted over to the hat and trotted right back to me carrying it proudly in her mouth. Hanna had chosen me to be her master.

She wasn't the perfect dog right away. It took almost five months before she was entirely housebroken and socialized. One day everything just seemed to click. Canids are extremely observant. From eight weeks of age until Hanna realized her place in the grand scheme

138

of things we were seldom more than 20 feet apart.

By the following September she was ready to hunt. There was a 10 acre sunflower field not far from home with a couple of tall, dead elms along one fence line which doves attacked with a vengeance.

Hanna and I would sit along this fence line facing each other almost every evening. When she saw doves approaching her ears would cock forward, brown eyes dancing in anticipation. Hanna knew what it meant when she heard the click on that Browning's safety. She also learned to watch my eyes.

If she didn't see birds but noticed my body tense she would automatically look back over her shoulder and get ready for action.

Hanna was also a great waterfowl dog. When she was five years old Cal, Dan and I planned a hunting/fishing trip around Devil's Lake, North Dakota. Dan's yellow Lab Maggie Moo Magnum had a medical issue and couldn't make the trip.

Hanna was not overly keen on traveling in a kennel instead of her rightful place on the front seat when we left for this trip, but she was able to endure these deplorable conditions for the greater good.

We were on I-90 about halfway through Minnesota with me at the wheel and Dan snoring happily in the backseat when Cal broke out his video camera to chronicle our adventure.

He panned back toward Dan, jowls fluttering with every exhalation. "Whaddya, think of that?" Cal asked.

"I think it's rare to see one with jowls that big this far south," I replied. Cal's spontaneous laughter found us tittering almost to Fargo.

Hanna acted as if this adventure was a four man trip, displaying every indication of being on equal footing with the two legged hunters. She made dozens of retrieves that week, with all but one duck delivered to hand without a feather out of place.

One diving duck that Cal knocked down back in the tules produced the sole act of defiance in Hanna's entire hunting career. Maybe she figured she deserved a break after making a dozen flawless retrieves. Perhaps the duck had an offensive scent.

She brought this black-and-white webfoot back towards where we waited in the weeds with less than her usual enthusiasm, stopping about 20 yards away on a mud flat and spitting the duck out on the ground.

Hanna then looked at me with what we all agreed was an evil grin and tore a big chunk out of the dead duck's breast!

Of course Dan and Cal thought this was hilarious. So much for my perpetual bragging that Hanna Banana was the perfect dog.

I waded angrily over to where she stood in defiance, grabbed the dead duck by its neck and slapped her with its carcass several times, coupled with loud and severe verbal reproach.

Except for working out a little too far after running pheasants a time or two this was the only mistake she ever made in the field.

Just when Hanna was coming into her absolute prime as a hunting dog my interest in bird hunting began to fade, with bowhunting a newfound passion. On of life's biggest regrets is robbing this companion of her best two working years. I've tried to make it up to her ever since.

Hanna is 9 ½ as these words are written—a Kim Basinger blond with caramel eyes. She is a little stiff in the morning now or after getting out of the truck after a long ride. Even walking through the woods looking for shed antlers in the spring sees her tuckering out after just a couple of hours, but being out there by my side is still the center of her universe.

There will be a day in the not too distant future that the fire will eventually go out of her eyes. This terrible day may still be a couple years down the road, but I'm absolutely devastated knowing of its undeniable approach.

Eventually Hanna will be laid to rest near the edge of the deck where she has spent so many days waiting for me to return from guiding or the deer woods before running up to celebrate return of the pack to full strength.

I will not be able to give her a warrior's farewell. I'm afraid the scene would turn into a murder-suicide. I love the dog that much. This and the fact that it wouldn't be fair to saddle another Lab with a master pushing legs too tired to hunt all day are why Hanna Banana is my last dog.

Too bad a man's life can't always end with dignity, put quietly down when continuing on brings more pain than joy. Hanna is looking up at me now, sensing something is wrong. Time to stop writing for awhile.

About The Author

Ted Peck grew up in Carroll County, Illinois with unquench-able passion for the outdoors that continues to drive his life today.

After graduating Southern Illinois University with a journal-ism degree in 1973 Peck found work as editor of a weekly newspaper in Durand, Illinois. He penned his first outdoor column in June of that year and has written at least one outdoor column or magazine article every week since that time.

A career as a professional firefighter for the City of Beloit, Wisconsin which began in 1979 provided ample opportunity to spend time hunting, fishing and writing about these pursuits. Peck was a paramedic for over 15 years as part of this job, retiring with the rank of lieutenant in 2001.

Shortly thereafter Peck and his wife Candy moved a little far-ther upstream and closer to the Mississippi River which has played a major role in this self-professed River Rat's life.

He continues to write regularly for newspapers and maga-zines, also working as a full time fishing guide on the River, a perpetual adventure which Peck has been enjoying for 38 years –and counting.

Made in the USA
Monee, IL
22 December 2021

86946208R00085